A PRIMER ON
MODERN-WORLD
ARCHAEOLOGY

PRINCIPLES OF ARCHAEOLOGY

ADVISORY EDITORS

Robert L. Bettinger, *University of California, Davis*
Gary M. Feinman, *The Field Museum, Chicago, Illinois*

A PRIMER ON MODERN–WORLD ARCHAEOLOGY
Charles E. Orser, Jr.

A PRIMER ON MODERN-WORLD ARCHAEOLOGY

CHARLES E. ORSER, JR.

Vanderbilt University
Nashville, Tennessee

ELIOT WERNER PUBLICATIONS, INC.
CLINTON CORNERS, NEW YORK

Library of Congress Cataloging-in-Publication Data

Orser, Charles E.
A primer on modern-world archaeology / Charles E. Orser, Jr., Vanderbilt
University, Nashville, Tennessee.
pages cm
Includes bibliographical references and index.
ISBN 978-0-9898249-2-7
1. Archaeology and history. 2. Globalization. I. Title.
CC77.H5O785 2014
930.1 – dc23

2013050486

ISBN-10: 0-9898249-2-6
ISBN-13: 978-0-9898249-2-7

Copyright © 2014 Eliot Werner Publications, Inc.
PO Box 268, Clinton Corners, New York 12514
http://www.eliotwerner.com

Printed in the United States of America

PREFACE

What exactly is modern-world archaeology and why do we need it? This primer seeks to answer these questions in clear and concise terms.

Modern-world archaeology, as I define it, is a kind of historical archaeology of the past five centuries that has as one of its main goals the analysis and interpretation of the union of the four great metaprocesses (or haunts) of modernity: colonialism, capitalism, Eurocentrism, and racialization. Modern-world archaeology is not simply historical archaeology focused on post-Columbian history, as some archaeologists have mistakenly concluded. The four haunts may have been born before 1492, but what makes the modern era unique is the way in which the four were harnessed together after the first Columbian expedition. Colonialists, capitalists, Eurocentrists, and racializers were innovative in creating overarching ways of expressing the super-processes of modernity. They were so persuasive and powerful that all four are still with us today.

I present here the most important themes of modern-world archaeology, beginning with its theoretical foundations. In the process I explain the differences between modern-world archaeology and traditional historical archaeology. I provide brief explorations of the four haunts and explain the importance of understanding the concept of structures. I also discuss the place of microhistory in modern-world archaeology and explore the special ways in which modern-world archaeologists perceive artifacts. Finally, I present some of the challenges facing modern-world archaeology in the twenty-first century.

This primer is an abbreviated reconsideration of modern-world archaeology as I first presented it in *A Historical Archaeology of the Modern World*, published in 1996. I have continuously thought about modern-world archaeology since then and have published a few short statements about my thinking in various journal articles and book chapters. This primer, however, is the first time since 1996 that I have offered a full, up-dated restatement of modern-world archaeology.

Readers familiar with the earlier book will notice that the greatest mod-ification I have made in this reconsideration is that I have substituted racial-ization for modernity. This change is the result of research I conducted for two books on the archaeology of race that I wrote after 1996. After much thought I decided that "modernity" has too broad a meaning to be entirely useful and that I could no longer overlook the historical and cultural sig-nificance of racialization as a meta-process of post-Columbian history. A strong element of this realization derived from acknowledging that the racialization process involves more than simple physical characteristics, and can include cultural variables as well.

The ideas I express in this book have evolved through interactions with various archaeologists and historians over the past few years. I have agreed with many of their theoretical positions, but not all of them. My disagree-ments with their ideas, however, have significantly strengthened my own thinking. In fact, comments made by skeptics have been tremendously helpful because by pointing out the weaknesses they have spurred me to rethink and refine my positions. I would like to thank the editors for agree-ing to include this primer in their series, and I would especially like to thank Kelly Dixon. Her suggestions and comments have helped me pro-vide clearer arguments.

The *Modern World* book developed in consultation with Eliot Werner, then archaeology editor at Plenum Press (which has since become Kluwer/Academic and now Springer). Even though he is not an archaeol-ogist, Eliot has always had a keen eye for what is important in archaeo-logical research. He helped shepherd some of the most important archaeological texts through the publication process beginning in the late 1970s, and archaeology would be much worse off without his efforts. Eliot encouraged me to write the *Modern World* book as the inaugural volume in a new series I was to edit for Plenum entitled Contributions to Global His-torical Archaeology. Eliot and I shared a vision for the future of historical archaeology as a truly global endeavor and the success of the series has proven him correct. He was also a guiding force behind the original idea, development, and first publication of the *International Journal of Historical Archaeology*, which as of this writing is just beginning its eighteenth year. Given this important archaeological history, I am proud to have this primer appear under his imprint.

CONTENTS

1 • Modern-World Archaeology **1**
Frames 2
Historical Archaeology : Modern-World Archaeology 5
   The Development of a Historical Archaeology 7
   Why Modern-World Archaeology? 9
   An Irish Example 11
Two Major Research Themes 13
   Culture Contact 14
   Social Inequality 16
Conclusion 19
Suggested Readings 21
Study Questions 22

2 • The Haunts **23**
The Meaning of the Haunts 23
A Brief Example 25
Colonialism 27
The Capitalist Project 29
   Mercantilism and Capitalism 31
   Globalization 33
Eurocentrism 35
Racialization 37
The Confluence of the Haunts in the Modern World 39
Suggested Readings 41
Study Questions 44

3 • The Foundation **45**
Structural History 45
   Braudel's Model 46
   Braudel and the Modern World 49
   Braudel's Structures 50

Network Theory   51
    Social Network Theory.   53
    Social Interaction.   56
    Network Units of Analysis   57
    Summary   60
World-Systems Analysis   61
    Frank's World Systems Theory   61
    Wallerstein's World-System Analysis.   63
    Summary   65
Dialectical Thinking.   66
    Marx's Dialectics   67
    Summary   69
Conclusion.   69
Suggested Readings.   70
Study Questions   72

4 • Structures   73
Epochal Structures   73
Epochal Structures and Human Agency.   74
    The Maale's Structures   76
A Brief Example from the Southern United States   77
    Antebellum Plantation Structures   77
    Dual Structures   80
Epochal Structures and the Haunts.   81
    Racism.   82
Conclusion.   83
Suggested Readings.   85
Study Questions   85

5 • Microhistory.   87
Some Archaeological History   88
    Archaeology and the Problem of Scale   89
The Essences of Microhistory   91
    Ginzburg's Microhistory   92
    Microhistory and the Lower Orders.   93
    Microhistory and Colonial America.   94
    Microhistory and the Importance of Social Networks.   97
Does Microanalysis Contain Any Dangers for Historical
    Archaeology?   98
Suggested Readings. 100
Study Questions 100

6 • Artifacts. 101
Archaeology's Enchantment with Objects 102
    Artifacts as Relational Objects. 103

The Distinction of Modern-World Artifacts 105
    Racialization and Access to Material Things 106
    The Role of Production....................................... 107
The Nature of Commodities..................................... 108
Value... 110
    Kinds of Value 111
The Social Imperatives of Artifacts-as-Commodities 112
    The Diderot Unity 113
    The Diderot Unity in Modern-World Archaeology 114
Taste 116
    Taste and Power.. 117
Suggested Readings 118
Study Questions 119

7 • Challenges 121
The Modern World... 122
Postcolonialism.. 123
    Defining Postcolonialism.................................... 124
    Four Elements of Postcolonial Analysis...................... 125
    New Ideas in Archaeology................................... 126
Separation 128
Acknowledging, Understanding, and Challenging the Haunts 129
    Capitalism 129
    Eurocentrism 132
    Racialization... 136
Conclusion.. 140
Suggested Readings.. 141
Study Questions 143

8 • The Future of Modern-World Archaeology 145
Why Is Relevance So Central? 146
    Is the Modern World Too Recent?........................... 147
    The Special Ability of Modern-World Archaeology........... 148
Final Thoughts 150
    The Challenges Ahead 152
Suggested Readings.. 152
Study Questions 153

References.. 155

Index 159

CHAPTER 1

MODERN-WORLD ARCHAEOLOGY

This primer provides a short introduction to the basic tenets and principles of modern-world archaeology. Modern-world archaeology is a specific approach to historical archaeology that explicitly investigates the post-1500 world through the lens of interconnectedness and interrelationships. Its broadest outlook is global, but its overt adherence to multiscalar analysis means that its practitioners have the freedom to extend their studies from the local to the global depending upon their interests and research questions.

The basic idea behind this book is that historical archaeology, as it is practiced around the world today, has now matured enough for us to begin to imagine another kind of historical archaeology—a modern-world archaeology that uses our acquired knowledge to take our research deeper into what it means to be "modern." One of the central tenets of modern-world archaeology is that the world we inhabit today is undeniably the product of the past five centuries. We cannot develop a full appreciation of our own time without having the wisdom to comprehend the many worlds our ancestors created. This history—like our own time—contains stories of struggle and success, hardship and ease, heroism and greed, played out over various time scales and geographical spaces.

Modern-world archaeology is not an academic exercise divorced from the realities of daily life. Quite the contrary, the archaeology of the most recent centuries has the unique ability to illuminate and explain the social and material realities of our own time. Modern-world archaeology offers exciting possibilities for the future but many of its threads are controversial. As a result not every practicing archaeologist will accept it. Practitioners who are engaged purely in artifact research or detailed site-specific studies may not find much here that will interest them; I ask them, however, to keep an open mind. It is completely acceptable that not everyone will adopt the goals or scope of modern-world archaeology. Many archaeologists will prefer to concentrate on the purely local or infinitely small,

1

and this is fine. For me this kind of research will always be the starting point rather than the end of the investigative process. I believe that only by broadening the field to the widest extent possible will historical archaeology reach its full potential as an anthropological practice.

In the following chapters, I present various topics that form the foundational thinking of modern-world archaeology. These topics include the importance of the four "haunts" of modernity, the role of microhistorical analysis in global studies, the significance of understanding epochal structures, and the central place of artifacts-as-commodities within modern-world archaeology. I also consider some of the challenges facing modern-world archaeologists in the twenty-first century.

FRAMES

A primary concept underlying these topics is the understanding that the world in which we now live, as well as that within which our ancestors lived, is composed of various complex scales (or frames) linking—at the widest—the local and the global. In his book *The Dynamics of Global Dominance: European Overseas Empires, 1415–1980*, David Abernethy perfectly described this method using the metaphor of a photographer adjusting a camera's zoom lens.

> Imagine a photographer focusing on the broad outlines of a large object located far away in order to learn something about the object. The photographer then twists the zoom lens to obtain a more detailed, higher-resolution image of a selected part of the distant object. As a result something new is observed through greater attention to the part's details. The zoom lens may be adjusted further to permit more precise examination of an even smaller part of the object. Each adjustment permits a novel visualization of reality by enabling the observer to come closer to whatever is being observed, in a subjective if not literal sense. For this reason each twist of the zoom lens can generate a new description of reality and perhaps new ideas to account for what the lens adjustment has revealed. (2000, p. 31)

Using this approach, we might imagine a photographer standing in a field of wildflowers with a camera equipped with a micro-macro zoom lens. The photographer can focus on a single flower or even one part of a single flower, but in the very next moment can photograph the entire field of flowers. He or she can even take a series of shots at various medium ranges, and all without moving. The flowers lose their individuality in the wide view but the picture of the field has little content without them. The individual flowers create the image, but how we see them depends upon our analytical frame. The same is true of archaeological analysis. How and what we interpret depends upon the frames we employ. I refer to the method used by the photographer, and the modern-world archaeologist, as the "sliding frame" approach (Figure 1).

The conscious acknowledgment that various frames exist in the modern world challenges us to sharpen our connections between both our immediate ancestors' pasts and our own times. Archaeologists have unique

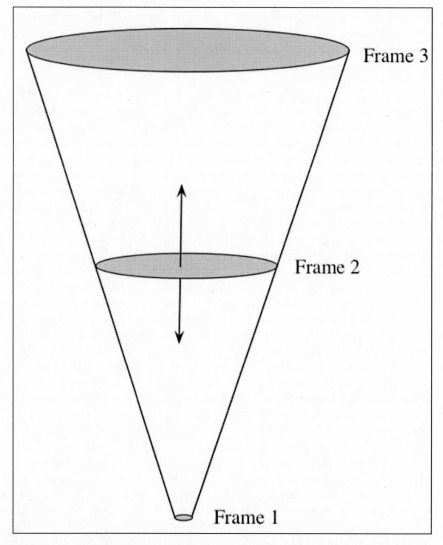

Figure 1. The "sliding frame" model.

abilities to provide to the present otherwise unknowable information about the past. Modern-world archaeologists investigate how forces far beyond our control can affect our physical surroundings and the objects we use everyday. Archaeologists studying all periods of history, even the most remote, know that human life in the absence of material things is impossible. Those of us living in the so-called "post-industrial West," with its runaway consumerism, should be especially aware of our acute desire for things. Using such knowledge, modern-world archaeologists can gauge how the wider world may be reflected by the actions we take within our own homes. The intricate interplay between the earth's specific localities and the globalized world is one of the most important subjects of modern-world archaeology.

To give a brief example. The invention of the smart phone has dramatically changed our lives in ways that were once unimaginable. We can check email, update our personal web pages, download music, play games, and do thousands of tasks no matter where we are on the planet. None of this was possible just twenty years ago. But how often do we think about the ways in which these little marvels have changed other elements of our material culture? Today not only do we have the smart phone itself, but we also have carrying cases, ear buds, screen protectors, and rechargers. The smart phone has also changed our behavior. Now, when we need to contact someone, we do not have to search to find a public phone (and, once found, determine whether it works, has a phonebook if we need it, and then hope we have the correct change). We now have our list of contacts as well as the entire Internet at our fingertips. The smart phone has also altered our appearance. Many people clip it to their side or attach it to their ear. Some people have learned to walk down busy streets while checking their email and the most adventurous claim that they can text while driving. (In June 2010 the Pew Research Center reported that 49% of survey respondents said they were in a car when the driver received or sent a text.) Smart phones, like many new technologies, have added words to our language as well. Until a few years ago, "text" was only a noun!

Drinking tea in the eighteenth century had a similar impact on people's daily lives. This great Chinese discovery, today a necessity for millions of people around the world, revolutionized the European colonial and continental worlds as much as the smart phone. For one thing, if you were to consume tea in the most fashionable way, you needed a special set of objects. To prepare and consume tea in the "proper" manner—to perform the English tea ceremony—required teapots, teacups, saucers, sugar bowls, tea towels, tongs, and strainers. In addition, the most fashionable hostess in the upper-class Anglo world would die of shame without an exquisite round table—preferably made of mahogany—on which to serve the tea. Concurrent with these special accouterments, many people decided that their tea tasted better sweetened, and so the demand for sugar skyrocketed.

The simple act of drinking tea, conducted in countless homes throughout Britain, colonial America, and elsewhere, had substantial global ramifications. Tea drinking was directly linked to New World slavery because enslaved people produced sugar under brutal plantation regimes. As the practice of drinking tea grew, Chinese (and later Indian) tea linked together Europe, North America, the Caribbean, and Africa. It also caused the significant expansion of a global network of mercantilist and capitalist exchange, as various European superpowers sought to control the world's shipping lanes and thus corner the markets for sugar, tea, and spices (and coffee, as well).

The archaeology of the modern world has the ability to illuminate an inherently complex and infinitely intriguing global history through its explicit interest in the diverse connections between the local and the global. These researches, when compiled, will help us understand the worlds in which our ancestors lived and allow us to relate them to our own times. The distance between eighteenth century tea drinking and twenty-first century smart phone usage is not as great as we might think.

Before delving more deeply into the basics of modern-world archaeology, a brief overview of historical archaeology is in order. This information, though much of it is well known, is worth reintroducing because it helps distinguish modern-world archaeology from traditional historical archaeology.

HISTORICAL ARCHAEOLOGY : MODERN–WORLD ARCHAEOLOGY

By the start of the twenty-first century, archaeologists had agreed on two definitions of historical archaeology. Under the first definition, archaeologists defined historical archaeology as a text-aided archaeology, meaning that its practitioners employed both excavated finds and documentary information in relatively equal measure. The methodology of the field was neither just archaeology (relying solely on systematic excavation) nor simply history (relying on written documents and other accounts of the past).

Archaeologists using this definition said that historical archaeology was exactly what the name implied: an archaeology with a "duo-disciplinary" method, with the two disciplines being archaeology and history. This broad definition meant that Egyptologists could be considered to be practicing historical archaeology, because they excavated tombs and temples and used the collected information in conjunction with the hieroglyphics they found chiseled onto ancient walls. Classical archaeologists could also be considered historical archaeologists because they used the same duo-disciplinary method; the ancient Greek texts they read were analogous to the hieroglyphics of ancient Egypt. Howard Carter—the famous discoverer of King Tut—and Heinrich Schliemann, who claimed he had discovered the ancient city of Troy using clues from Homer's *Iliad*, can be considered early historical archaeologists under this definition.

The definition of historical archaeology as a discipline that relies equally on sources from history and archaeology is inherently true. All historical archaeologists, regardless of where they choose to excavate, examine written texts and excavated materials with each of their research endeavors. In addition to what we might normally think of as "historical" texts—written documents—historical archaeologists also make extensive use of maps and plans, oral histories and the memories of living men and women, photographs, drawings, and just about any other source useful for shedding light on an archaeological investigation. Perhaps all historical archaeologists, despite their particular specialties, would agree that they regularly and happily use the duo-disciplinary approach all the time. In fact, this is one of the strengths of text-aided archaeology. (Most historical archaeologists would probably also add that they use a multidisciplinary approach, though archaeological and historical sources would undoubtedly be most prominent among the many sources they consult.)

The equation of historical archaeology with text-aided archaeology is accurate, but most archaeologists who self-identify as historical archaeologists would probably say that text-aided archaeology only defines their methodology; it does not describe their historical interests. If surveyed, most historical archaeologists today would probably agree that while they use many sources of information to study the past—excavation most uniquely—their focus of interest begins sometime around the year 1500 and continues forward from there. In other words, most of today's historical archaeologists would say that their field is more than just a method for studying history. They would propose that they investigate a particular segment of history, the past five hundred years, a period we can term "modern history" if we wish.

The idea that historical archaeology is the archaeology of a specific era first gained acceptance in the 1970s when two archaeologists, Robert Schuyler and James Deetz, defined the field as the study of the spread of European cultures into the world beginning around 1500 and continuing into the present. As archaeologists in the United States, their intent was to separate North American prehistory from history, with the dividing line being the presence of Europeans and all the things they brought with them to the New World. These introductions included literacy, an unfamiliar collection of material things, infectious diseases, and new forms of social and political life. The distinction between American Indian archaeology and the archaeology of Europeans provided a way for the earliest professional historical archaeologists to distinguish themselves within the wider field of archaeology—a field in which they were a distinct, and not always appreciated, minority.

The goal of separating time into two large segments was important because most professional historical archaeologists had been trained in pre-European contact American Indian archaeology (though some were experts in the related fields of historical architecture and restoration, while others were completely self-taught). Many archaeologists today are skeptical that a concrete break occurred between prehistory and history, but the division made sense in the 1970s because it helped establish the professionalism of historical archaeology as a distinct kind of archaeological practice. This work was important during a time when American historical archaeologists were struggling to be recognized as serious scholars. Sadly, this struggle continues in those places where post-1500 historical archaeology is a relatively new pursuit. In general, the study of the very ancient or spectacular continues to have the most cachet to the profession as well as to the general public.

The Development of a Historical Archaeology

The earliest beginnings of the archaeology of the most recent five centuries occurred in the mid-nineteenth century, though not as a professional field of study. People interested in history as a hobby (whom we sometimes call "history buffs") began to probe around old forts, religious missions, and other historic places. Many of these individuals merely scratched in the earth for relics, but others were more serious excavators. Some of them realized that excavated artifacts could be perceived as tiny pieces of history similar to historical documents. The artifacts' messages could not be easily read like old manuscripts, but they nonetheless could be used as signposts to the past. As a result of this thinking, in 1855 Jesuit Father Félix Martin traveled to the backwoods of today's Ontario, Canada, to locate the long-abandoned site of Ste. Marie I, a mission to the Huron Indians begun in 1639 by members of his religious order. The following year James Hall dug around the Massachusetts home of Miles Standish, his famous ancestor who led the Pilgrims on the *Mayflower*. Other pioneering historical archaeologists searched river valleys and streambeds for ruined trading posts and the remnants of forts and colonial settlements.

The work of these early archaeological explorers did not lead directly to the development of historical archaeology as a scholarly field of study, and little concrete information often exists to document their efforts. Most of them were not employed as archaeologists, so their often-extensive collections of artifacts and notes were frequently lost or discarded after their deaths.

It was not until the 1930s that historical archaeology as a discipline was practiced in the United States. Some of this research was purely scholarly, with the archaeologist using excavation as a tool of historical inquiry. Much of the early research at religious missions in California was conducted in this vein. By far the most important studies conducted in the United States during the earliest history of historical archaeology occurred as part of a New Deal program designed to interpret sites and properties, with the goal of promoting nationalism and tourism. Excavation at Jamestown, Virginia, for example, was one such effort. Projects such as these were usually not conducted in accordance with present-day archaeological standards. Nonetheless, these research efforts—generally performed with the proper spirit in mind—set the stage for the full-scale development of historical archaeology into the professional pursuit it is today.

As a professional endeavor with its own scholarly journals, historical archaeology only dates to the late 1960s. At this time archaeologists dedicated to the study of post-1500 history developed two journals: *Historical Archaeology*, the official journal of the Society for Historical Archaeology (SHA); and *Post-Medieval Archaeology*, the journal of the Society for Post-Medieval Archaeology (SPMA). The societies' names were largely a function of where they were located, with the SHA being largely a North American society and the SPMA being based in Great Britain. At the time North American archaeologists tended to make the distinction between prehistory and history, but members of the SPMA could not make this neat division because the British Isles had much longer written histories. British historical archaeologists thus tended to separate medieval history (approximately 1100–1400) from post-medieval history (1400–1750), even though both medieval and post-medieval archaeologists could realistically be considered historical archaeologists because they excavated and studied historical texts.

For this reason, then, what in the United States would be termed "historical archaeology" (and sometimes even "colonial archaeology") became "post-medieval archaeology" in Great Britain (and eventually throughout the rest of Europe). The terms are deceptive, however, because both American-trained historical archaeologists and British-trained post-medieval archaeologists study the same topics using the same methods (as do continentally trained post-medieval archaeologists). As a demonstration of their shared interests, the SHA and the SPMA occasionally hold joint annual conferences where the attendees discuss subjects of trans-Atlantic interest.

The journals of the SHA and the SPMA were joined in 1983 by *Australasian Historical Archaeology* and in 1997 by the *International Journal of Historical Archaeology*. Since the 1980s more areal and regional societies have regularly held professional conferences and created journals dedicated to post-1500 historical archaeology. (In eastern North America, the Council for Northeast Historical Archaeology—including archaeologists from the United States and Canada—had been created as early as 1966, before the formal institution of either the SHA or the SPMA.) By the dawn of the twenty-first century, historical archaeology was arguably the fastest growing kind of archaeology being practiced internationally. Today archaeologists interested in post-1500 history conduct research in every corner of the world.

Why Modern-World Archaeology?

Many historical archaeologists well versed in their discipline's history already know much of this information and I have explored it elsewhere as well. I believe, however, that many historical archaeologists just coming into the field do not fully appreciate the history of their discipline, even though as theorists they collectively portray a sophistication unknown to the early history of the field. Failure to acknowledge the discipline's development makes it difficult to understand the need for modern-world archaeology. In other words, why is an explicit modern-world archaeology needed when it is clear that most people who self-identify as historical archaeologists study post-1500 history exclusively?

I use the term "modern-world archaeology" to separate the study of the most recent centuries (the second and more widely used definition of historical archaeology) from the method (the first, broader definition). My use of modern-world archaeology is similar in many ways to the earlier but now-disused term "historic sites archaeology." Robert Schuyler defined this term as "the study of the material manifestation of the expansion of European culture into the non-European world starting in the 15th century and ending with industrialization or the present depending on local conditions" (1970, p. 84). A similar term, "historic site archaeology" (with no "s"), was mostly used by historical archaeologists in the southeastern United States from 1960 to 1982.

Important distinctions exist, however, between historic sites archaeology and modern-world archaeology. For one thing, the focus of modern-world archaeology need not be specifically on Europeans; modern-world archaeologists most certainly investigate indigenous life. Contrary to the view of some critics, modern-world archaeology is not and has never been designed as Eurocentric (see Chapter 2). That said, however, archaeologists who claim to be practicing modern-world archaeology cannot overlook or ignore the myriad impacts Europeans have had upon the native peoples whose historical lives they study. A myopic investigation of a native culture, devoid of any mention of European contact, is historical archaeology rather than modern-world archaeology. As noted above, modern-world archaeology is inherently relational in outlook, and some of the most far-reaching relationships that were enacted in the post-1500 world involved native peoples and Europeans.

Another difference between historic sites archaeology and modern-world archaeology is that the latter explicitly offers a critique of modernity as one of its prime motivations. Modernity continues to the present ("postmodernity" being an empty concept created for political reasons), and a modern-world archaeologist seeks to use the special insights and methods of historical archaeology to address social and cultural issues of relevance both to the present and the past.

Given the differences between historical archaeology, historic sites archaeology, and modern-world archaeology, from this point forward I will use "historical archaeology" or "traditional historical archaeology" to refer to the duo-disciplinary method, and to archaeology concentrated on post-1500 history but without the focus of modern-world archaeology. An examination of eighteenth century New York City that fails to mention the relationships between racial classification and settlement locale, for example, might constitute an excellent piece of scholarship in historical archaeology, but the research cannot be considered modern-world archaeology if the archaeologist fails to consider how housing segregation continued in the nineteenth and twentieth centuries (and how such discrimination continues into the present).

Numerous archaeologists have adequately demonstrated that archaeology, of whatever period of history, is never simply about the past. Most archaeologists in the not-too-distant past denied this simple tenet of today's archaeology (see Chapter 7). The acknowledgment of concrete present : past connections is especially relevant to modern-world archaeology because its interests extend by definition into the present. The things with which we surround ourselves today provide strong connections to the past and tie modern-world archaeology to anthropological studies of present-day consumerism, consumption, and globalization. The examination of consumerism alone gives modern-world archaeology a vibrancy that makes it uniquely relevant to present-day society in interesting and profound ways.

One of the greatest strengths of historical and modern-world archaeology is the ability to reveal the hidden histories of individuals and communities that have been ignored, forgotten, poorly represented, and even misrepresented in and by documentary history. Much of the research conducted during the earliest years of professional historical archaeology focused on the rich and famous, with the sites of interest generally being the homes of colonial elites, eminent politicians, and notable pioneers or military sites associated with celebrated battles, campaigns, and leaders. Today's historical archaeology has moved away from the exclusive study of the powerful and historical archaeologists are justifiably proud of their research into the lives of the less famous, the historically ignored, and the socially powerless. Some of the most interesting research being conducted today concentrates on the lives of convicts, soldiers, rural tenant farmers, sufferers of Hanson's disease, urban slum dwellers, immigrants, and prostitutes.

We know from historians that such people existed in the past (just as they do today) but the documentation about them might be sketchy, biased, or simply unavailable. Historical archaeology provides a way to illuminate the daily lives of the enslaved, immigrants, rural farmers, coal miners, and illiterate canal diggers, using excavation to provide the unique and highly personal information chroniclers of the past seldom transcribed in their notebooks. Such studies help illuminate strategies for survival, personal freedom, and enfranchisement within social environments that were often hostile. Historical archaeologists also conduct innovative, culturally sensitive studies of indigenous life, often completed in collaboration with members of descendant communities themselves. These studies, conducted throughout the world, enrich our appreciation of the cultural lives of non-Europeans in dramatic and exciting ways.

Scope is one place that modern-world archaeology and historical archaeology diverge. If archaeologists conducting a detailed study of a particular site, neighborhood, or region carry the perspective forward into a consideration of larger frames of analysis, they are practicing modern-world archaeology. If they do not make these broader connections, their work is historical archaeology. Many historical archaeologists, because they are interested in documenting past daily life as historical ethnographers, fail to relate their carefully crafted descriptions to the larger world. Historical archaeologists who work only on one scale do nothing wrong. In fact, some of the most important studies present concrete information about life in a single place during one period of history. These particular examinations can provide a richness of detail that resonates with people living today, and they are significant tools in furthering the discipline's commitment to use archaeological research to deepen the public's interest in and knowledge of human history. But these studies cannot be considered modern-world archaeology unless the archaeologist also explores the impacts of the wider world on the site's inhabitants.

An Irish Example

My own research in County Roscommon, Ireland, provides a useful illustration. During the summers between 1997 and 2001 inclusive, my students and I excavated two house remains in the townland of Ballykilcline (Figure 2). (A townland is an administrative unit composed of houses and fields but no shops or services.) An extensive documentary record indicated that over five hundred people once lived on the townland and worked as tenant farmers, raising potatoes for food. The village was created around 1800; the tenants began a rent strike in 1834 and in 1847–1848 all but three families were forcibly evicted.

Our archaeological data—combined with evidence collected from other contemporary sites excavated in counties Sligo and Donegal, and elsewhere in County Roscommon—documented that the families obtained abundant English-made refined ceramics, even though they were widely perceived as mere "peasants." As peasants, so goes the argument, they were not supposed to have objects similar to those that historical archae-

Figure 2. Excavation at Ballykilcline, Ireland.

ologists have found elsewhere throughout the nineteenth century world. An archaeologist conducting an excavation at an early nineteenth century site in rural New York would not have been surprised by any of the ceramics we discovered in rural Ireland. Peasants, particularly those living in central Ireland, were expected to possess only the objects they had fashioned themselves from wood and straw using time-honored, traditional methods. But such was not the case; they were tied into a huge network.

Our research at Ballykilcline could be considered an example of historical archaeology because we used common archaeological methods, combined with historical information, to reveal and describe a slice of history. Surprisingly little information about the material culture of early nineteenth century rural Ireland existed prior to our excavations. As was the case with enslaved Africans in the Americas, most of the information about nineteenth century rural Irish tenant farmers was present in written history or buried in folk memory. Our research illuminated an aspect of lived history that was poorly understood and, though much remains to be accomplished, it has begun the process of writing accurate historical ethnographies of a people about whom little concrete information exists.

Our research could not be considered an example of modern-world archaeology if our inquiry ceased at Ballykilcline's boundaries. Such a restrictive approach would have made it virtually impossible to understand the people's historical circumstances and sociohistorical milieu. Our research had to move beyond the townland frame. As tenant farmers the townland's residents were enmeshed in a system that was neither of their making nor their choosing. The tenant farming system was inherently oppressive because it allowed large landowners, many of whom were absentees living elsewhere in Great Britain, to set rents and imprison or evict those who did not or could not pay them. After 1834, when the rent strike began, the tenants of Ballykilcline had perhaps the most renowned landlady of all: Princess Victoria, crowned queen of the British Empire in 1837 when the rent strike was only in its third year. Many of the forces that helped shape the people's lives originated far beyond their townland's borders. The people undoubtedly had some degree of freedom within their daily lives, but we cannot overlook the reality that they were controlled from cradle to grave by the tenancy system—as well as by the laws the British Parliament saw fit to impose upon them.

It would be entirely possible to approach the situation at Ballykilcline as a brief moment in time that lasted from 1800 to 1848. An archaeological ethnography combining the abundant historical documentation with the archaeological findings would be valuable in its own right and would constitute an example of historical archaeology. But stopping the research at the local scale misses two significant elements that relate to the present day. First, a large group of direct descendants of the evictees—now living throughout the United States and Canada—have formed an organization called the Ballykilcline Society. These individuals care deeply about the history of the townland and the genealogies of their ancestors. The research conducted at the townland matters a great deal to these individuals.

Equally important, however, is a circumstance that gives places like Ballykilcline added meaning today. The beautiful green vistas promoted by the Irish Tourist Board, which millions of tourists visit Ireland every year to see, are really landscapes of dispossession. Where today we find lush green fields, romantic stone walls, and the occasional ruined abbey, we would once have found smoky villages teeming with life. The cruelties of the tenancy system, the Great Irish Famine, and emigration and widespread eviction created the landscape so many spend a lifetime waiting and saving to see. The adoption of a multiscalar perspective allows us to move effortlessly between present and past, the small and the large, and to envision the impacts of eviction in Ireland and throughout the world. The events in Ireland during the famine of the late 1840s were simultaneously local and global. Overlooking this fact does violence both to the past and to our perceptions of it in the present.

TWO MAJOR RESEARCH THEMES

The explosion in historical archaeology that began sometime in the late 1980s has meant that today it is difficult to enumerate the most actively pursued topics of study. Historical archaeologists around the world are researching innumerable topics that have relevance on many levels, extending from the minutely local to the broadly international, and their interests are as varied as the number of archaeologists. Of all the topics currently being studied by today's historical archaeologists, two of them stand in the forefront—as they have since the first days that archaeologists practiced what they termed "historical archaeology": culture contact and social inequality. These topics have direct relevance to modern-world archaeology, and in fact they help distinguish research in modern-world archaeology from traditional historical archaeology.

Culture Contact

The study of contact between disparate cultures has been an important research topic for historical archaeologists from the beginning and remains so today. In fact, it would be fair to say that much historical archaeology was originally designed—at least within American anthropology—specifically to study culture contact. Mid-twentieth century archaeologists who investigated native cultures at the time of their first contacts with Europeans quickly discovered that they knew little about the artifacts, buildings, and ways of life of the Europeans. This was ironic because of the two cultures it was the Europeans, not the Native Americans, who had written records. As anthropology students they had spent years learning to identify and date American Indian pottery, stone tools, and settlement patterns. However, they knew little about the European ceramics and glass, brass musket parts, and stone gunflints they found in their excavations. These early historical archaeologists also had little knowledge about the designs of the houses the European settlers had built in their forts and villages. Historians were adept at providing information about the broad sequence of colonial history but concrete evidence about the Europeans' dwellings, their conventions of trash disposal, their settlement patterns, and their personal possessions was sadly lacking.

The general lack of knowledge meant that much of the earliest research in historical archaeology was object driven: it involved becoming familiar with the objects and settlements of all those peoples who had come to the shores of North America as the continent's first European immigrants. Pioneering historical archaeologists throughout the once-colonized world had the same basic learning experience.

The first professional historical archaeologists understood that it would be unsatisfactory to focus on Europeans alone; they acknowledged that they had to understand how these immigrants interacted with the cultures with which they had come into contact. As a result the archaeological study of culture contact developed early as a major focus of research. Initially, much of this research usually portrayed a Eurocentric bias because the archaeologists (thinking only along one dimension) tended to wonder how European muskets, glass beads, and brass kettles had affected the natives who accepted and used these unfamiliar objects. The view that culture change occurred in only one direction—from "learned" Europeans to "less sophisticated" indigenous peoples—extended well into the 1960s and sometimes beyond.

Anthropologically trained historical archaeologists soon began to appreciate that culture change never occurs only in one direction; the changes wrought by contact affects both parties in various and often quite profound ways. This realization led to the development of questions centering on mutual exchange. Anthropologists have proven to archaeologists that people seldom accept foreign objects and new ways of life without modifying them or imbuing them with new, sometimes quite subtle meanings. Research on European : non-European contact has thus become a much more sophisticated and anthropologically relevant field of study than it was when historical archaeology began. Most archaeologists' research reports no longer contain page after page of artifact descriptions; their studies now reflect a greater interest in the cultural dynamics of the often rapidly changing social and natural environments that accompany culture contact.

Historical archaeologists today work at contact-era sites everywhere in the world and many are investigating the topic with vigor. Their efforts and insights are significantly broadening our understanding of the sociomaterial dimensions of contact and are creating ways to understand how its myriad legacies continue to affect our contemporary world.

By the end of the twentieth century, increasing numbers of archaeologists had begun explicitly to convert their studies of culture contact into investigations of postcolonialism and imperialism—topics that fit perfectly within the purview of modern-world archaeology (see Chapter 7). Whereas traditional historical archaeologists might view these phenomena neutrally, expressing dispassionate distance (or separation; see Chapter 8), modern-world archaeology is critical of colonialism and imperialism. It is not unusual, for example, to find many excellent studies of military installations in traditional historical archaeology. Readers of such studies can usually find precise details about the history, construction, and material culture of European forts, outposts, and blockhouses. They can learn just about everything they would ever wish to know about the particular place under study.

This kind of research is important to historical archaeology, but it cannot be considered an example of modern-world archaeology unless the archaeologist thinks in a multiscalar, multi-temporal manner and attempts to link the life and history of the fort with the wider world. It may indeed be true that life at the fort represents a "small world," but without a contextualization connecting the place with the dynamic histories of colonialism and capitalism, the work will never be more than an interesting example of single-site archaeology. Modern-world archaeology sees colonialism as forever linked in the post-1500 world with the capitalist project of global expansion.

Modern-world archaeologists, like many historical archaeologists, often seek to understand how indigenous peoples resisted or rejected the domination and oppression that so often accompanied culture contact. This focus helps archaeologists appreciate the often-direct historical connections between archaeology and colonialism and how archaeological findings can be used for unintended political purposes. The history of archaeology shows that the profession has frequently served the imperialist's goal of acquiring the cultural treasures of other peoples, and many museum curators living in former colonialist nation-states are today reevaluating the conditions under which their collections were amassed.

Most archaeologists working today are sensitive to issues of cultural patrimony. Principal among the reasons for this awareness is that many of the best researchers in the field—and certainly many historical archaeologists studying culture contact—regularly collaborate with indigenous scholars and cultural activists. These joint efforts deepen our understanding of culture contact and help elevate archaeological research into a socially responsible kind of scholarship, a goal that is perfectly consistent with modern-world archaeology. Such interactions teach us that many perspectives exist about the past. Historical and modern-world archaeologists involved in such collaborations are challenged to provide ways of being sensitive to the needs and desires of indigenous communities, while also being true to today's best archaeological standards.

Social Inequality

Historical archaeologists examining culture contact have an equal interest in the ways in which people in the past have been separated into distinct groups. Regardless of an archaeologist's individual theoretical perspective, all regularly use excavated artifacts, housing forms, and settlement patterns to investigate the social divisions that occurred in past human organizations. Historical archaeologists understand that social inequalities appear along many dimensions, with the most obvious being along the lines of class, gender, and perceived racial affiliation.

Many of the distinctions between peoples are unquestionably deep seated in history. The ancient Egyptians distinguished between peoples based on the color of their skin, and other cultures have similarly used physical attributes (e.g., hair color, eye contour, head shape) and cultural characteristics (e.g., clothing style, language, religion) to separate the mass of the world's peoples into distinct groups. And no matter how often scholars promote the idea that the only race on earth is the human race, the perception of physical appearance and cultural variation—defined as race—has been an ethnocentric mainstay for generations. Cultural historians and anthropologists go to great lengths to stress the commonality of all peoples, but social inequality continues to exist and thus is an important subject for historical archaeology and especially for modern-world archaeology.

For many years an individual's social status was widely perceived as relatively fixed. People generally understood social status as the totality of a person's attributes: education, family history, economic prosperity, ethnicity, and so forth. Archaeologists interpreted this idea to mean that it should be possible to locate certain artifacts that can be used to signal past social standing. Many historical archaeologists thus assumed that nineteenth century white clay smoking pipes impressed with shamrocks represented Irish ethnicity and that pieces of opium pipes were associated with Chinese immigrants. The search for these so-called "ethnic markers" constituted a significant portion of the historical archaeologist's social research from the late 1960s to the 1980s.

Beginning in the late 1980s, however, many historical archaeologists began to realize that the easy association of specific artifacts with past social standing was far too simplistic. Since then historical archaeologists have become much more sophisticated in their understanding of social position and have come to appreciate that a person's identity is complex enough to be situational—meaning that it can change with each social situation. A woman might be a bank manager, a mother, and a daughter all at the same time, but each of these social positions will be expressed in different ways depending upon the social context (i.e., with whom she is in contact). This understanding has made the archaeological study of social inequality much more difficult and the interpretations are likely to be presented more cautiously than in the past. Today historical archaeologists still intent on examining social status typically use the term to refer specifically to socioeconomics.

Some research in historical archaeology—particularly that associated with the study of ethnicity—often focuses on social cohesion rather than social inequality. Here a group's understanding of togetherness and belonging overrides any feelings of inferiority that might be imposed from outside the group. Such research often focuses on cultural survival and frequently overlaps with research on culture contact and resistance.

Research into the material culture of poverty constitutes one of the prime research interests of modern-world archaeology. Among the reasons for this interest are that (a) poverty has existed in the world for centuries, although its continued presence is particularly relevant to mercantilism and capitalism; (b) poverty continues to exist in the present and thus many of its conditions have historical roots; and (c) the material conditions of poverty are not well understood, especially by archaeologists.

One of the most interesting elements of poverty is its frequent linkage with racial identification. In the world colonized by Europeans beginning around 1500, the connection between race and poverty began with the earliest interactions between indigenous peoples and European newcomers.

Many of the tensions caused by the contact between these two social structures continue to exist in our present world. The specific manifestations of these connections and their meanings vary over short periods of time but are remarkably consistent when examined over the long term. Their consistency derives from the structural nature of the linkages rather than idiosyncratic practices or behaviors (see Chapter 5).

We must also remember that race is not ethnicity. Ethnicity refers to ways in which groups self-identify because of a shared notion of culture, heritage, and nation. Ethnicity is imposed from the inside. Race is imposed from the outside, typically by individuals who view themselves as superior and who have enough economic and cultural resources to be situated at the pinnacle of a society's social hierarchy. Ethnicity, though significant on personal and familial levels, loses importance on the societal level as various ethnic groups are racialized as part of the dominant ideology pressed upon them. Their involvement in the assignment of racial ranking is involuntary but unavoidable given the structural nature of the process. Racialized groups may tenaciously hold on to their ethnic expressions and attitudes, but these lose significance to—or are deemed insignificant by—those in power.

Poverty in the United States, like race, is structural because of the inherent inequalities associated with the capitalist paradigm. Poverty certainly existed before the rise of capitalism, but poverty has been one of capitalism's enduring features. Failure in capitalism is deemed wholly personal because the social contract created by capitalist practice assigns to individuals primary responsibility for economic success. The ideology of individualism embedded within capitalism, in masking the realities of the class hierarchy, maintains that everyone is born with the same inherent qualities and that equal opportunity for success exists for all. Failure, when it occurs, is the result of personal shortcoming.

Modern-world archaeology adopts a multiscalar and structural perspective to investigate poverty as a severe expression of social inequality. It accepts that poverty is an all-too-real hardship faced by millions of families around the globe. Confronted individually, responses to poverty can be idiosyncratic. Modern-world archaeology, in addition to investigating the limited individual and household frames, also examines the nature of capitalist accumulation at the largest frame. We all know that the material manifestations of wealth make it easier to identify certain men and women from the past, and that poverty has the power to hide those who experience it. The preservation of historical records and physical monuments built for and about the wealthy means that we know much more about them individually than we do about the millions of people who were humble and thus obscure in history. The ability of the well-to-do to mask the disadvantaged is one characteristic of hierarchical social structures, especially those that incorporate a mix of capitalist practice and racial categorization.

Poverty itself, however, is not easily defined. Archaeologists must devise ways to instill it with archaeological relevance. It would do archaeologists little good, for example, to focus on the psychological elements of poverty if they cannot identify and measure it in material terms. As a result, while we may well understand and fully accept the personal toll severe want can entail, we also must be cognizant at all times of the large-scale material dimensions of poverty—in addition to recognizing its individual and small-scale expressions. Fortunately, multiscalar analyses can do precisely this.

CONCLUSION

Historical archaeology is exploding as a field of study within the larger world of professional archaeology. As late as the 1970s—and in some places even today—far too many archaeologists believed that the serious study of fragmented gunflints, rusted horseshoes, and deteriorating medicine bottles from the recent past was unworthy of archaeological investigation. They believed that these artifacts and the people who produced, bought, sold, used, and discarded them were the exclusive domain of historians. These archaeologists tended to think that the only proper subject matter was indigenous peoples, preferably those without systems of writing.

Most professional archaeologists no longer think this way, and historical archaeology in the early twenty-first century is playing an increasingly significant role in interpreting the world's history and diverse cultural expressions. Many historians accept that written history leaves a great deal unsaid and that archaeology can both answer many specific questions and address social subjects of wide breadth. Without question practicing historical archaeologists will continue to discover important new sites and develop innovative insights about peoples whom we think we already know, as well as those whom we do not know at all. New university programs in historical archaeology are constantly being created at colleges and universities around the world, and historical archaeology is destined to become one of the most important fields of archaeological study.

In this book I start by assuming that historical archaeology has matured enough that we can now begin to think about expanding its focus to create another historical archaeology, a truly modern-world archaeology. The catalog of excavated sites is growing daily and our knowledge is expanding in new and important ways. The advances made over the past two decades alone mean that we can begin to construct broader ways of perceiving our research. As I explain later, the detailed investigation of specific sites will always be the mainstay of research in historical archaeology. But as I stress in the following chapters, I understand that historical archaeology—reconfigured as modern-world archaeology—has many significant contributions to make to our understanding of the worlds that existed beyond the single archaeological site. Our research methods and our ability to reveal hidden history provide a wonderful way for us to begin to understand our place, and our ancestors' places, in the world as it has been created following the transoceanic European voyages that began in earnest after 1492.

Table 1. Differences Between Historical Archaeology and Modern-World Archaeology

Feature	Historical archaeology	Modern-world archaeology
Focus	Literate history	Post-1500 CE world
Method	Multidisciplinary	Multidisciplinary
Perspective	Single scale, some multi-scalar	Multiscalar by definition
Use of time	Past → present	Earlier past ↔ past ↔ present
Scope	One site, neighborhood, region, some transnational	Local ↔ global
Theories	Eclectic	Structural history, network theory, world-systems theory, dialectics

Important distinctions occur between traditional historical archaeology and modern-world archaeology (Table 1). It is important to remember this adage: *all modern-world archaeology is historical archaeology, but not all historical archaeology is modern-world archaeology.* Modern-world archaeology strives to pick up where much historical archaeology ends. It seeks to investigate our own world through the lens of the past, rather than simply employing the platitude that we study the past to understand the present. Modern-world archaeology sees this differently. To understand our present, we must work back into the past to discover the historical roots of our times in order that we might—in the course of these investigations—discover ways to right the wrongs of the past and create a more just, equal world. Modern-world archaeology will be a success if it can do this in even the smallest ways.

SUGGESTED READINGS

World History

Abernethy, David B. 2000. *The Dynamics of Global Dominance: European Overseas Empires, 1415–1980*. Yale University Press, New Haven, CT.

Arrighi, Giovanni. 2010. *The Long Twentieth Century: Money, Power and the Origins of Our Times*. Verso, London.

Hart, Jonathan. 2008. *Empires and Colonies*. Polity Press, Cambridge, UK.

Marks, Robert B. 2002. *The Origins of the Modern World: A Global and Ecological Narrative*. Rowman and Littlefield, Lanham, MD.

Four books that provide overviews of global history, concentrating on post-Columbian history.

Russell-Wood, A. J. R. 1992. *The Portuguese Empire, 1415–1808: A World on the Move*. Johns Hopkins University Press, Baltimore, MD.

An excellent historical overview of the role of the Portuguese in creating the modern world. Provides wonderful examples of cultural interaction and exchange throughout the colonial world.

Historical Archaeology

Deetz, James. 1977. *In Small Things Forgotten: An Archaeology of Early American Life*. Anchor Doubleday, New York.

A famous introduction to historical archaeology written by one of its major figures. Not modern-world archaeology, but many of the author's ideas have influenced modern-world archaeology.

Orser, Charles E., Jr. 1996. *A Historical Archaeology of the Modern World*. Plenum Press, New York.

My earliest thinking about modern-world archaeology. Provides the foundation for the present book.

Schuyler, Robert L. 1970. Historical Archaeology and Historic Sites Archaeology as Anthropology: Basic Definitions and Relationships. *Historical Archaeology* 4:83–89.

An early exploration of the many connections between historical archaeology and anthropology.

STUDY QUESTIONS

1. Indicate some of the differences between traditional historical archaeology and modern-world archaeology. Why is it true that all modern-world archaeology is historical archaeology, but not all historical archaeology is modern-world archaeology?

2. Explain, in the context of modern-world archaeology, what is meant by "frames."

3. Think of an artifact that has changed the way you live. How would your life be different without it? Would it be better or worse?

4. Outline a research strategy for investigating culture contact or social inequality using a combination of archaeological and historical information as primary research tools.

CHAPTER 2

THE HAUNTS

The "haunts" constitute one of the central features of modern-world archaeology. Archaeologists who do not consider at least two of the haunts in their research cannot be practicing modern-world archaeology. This simple fact reinforces a central axiom mentioned in Chapter 1: that all modern-world archaeology is historical archaeology, but that not all historical archaeology is modern-world archaeology. Modern-world archaeologists adopt the transdisciplinary methods and sources of traditional historical archaeology (ranging from collecting personal reminiscences to measuring bore sizes of clay smoking pipe stems) and explore the same periods of history, but if they ignore the impacts of the haunts, they cannot be considered modern-world archaeologists.

The four haunts that constitute the central subject matter of modern-world archaeology are colonialism, mercantilism/capitalism, Eurocentrism, and racialization. I did not originally include racialization in my earliest explanation of modern-world archaeology, but I have sought to rectify this oversight in more recent work. I have also included mercantilism in my exploration of capitalism since our use of dialectical thinking (see Chapter 3) means that we cannot ignore capitalism's precursor. The development of capitalism was formed within mercantilism and mercantilism remains deeply rooted within capitalism. Too narrow a focus on capitalism per se, without explicitly considering its earlier incarnation, diminishes our ability to understand the full development of capitalist practice in the diverse sociohistorical contexts that have been created in the world since about 1500.

THE MEANING OF THE HAUNTS

The haunts are structurally complex and sociohistorically unique to the point that scholars have written shelves of books about each of them. Complexity, however, is no reason to shy away from them, and my explanations are presented with an eye toward establishing the archaeological relevance of each. My goals are (a) to demonstrate the significance of each haunt individually; (b) to illustrate their interconnectedness in the world since about 1500; and (c) to show their importance in the practice of contemporary archaeology. The haunts constitute simultaneous vertical and horizontal networks (see Chapter 3). People experienced them in various ways in the past, we feel their impacts in the present, and future generations will encounter them as well.

We must also appreciate that even though my discussions concentrate on their historical expressions, my use of the term "haunts" is theoretically informed by the four foundational concepts explained in Chapter 3. Some critics of my book *A Historical Archaeology of the Modern World* misinterpreted or misunderstood my use of this term. I meant it then, and I most certainly mean it now, to describe four meta-processes that operate in the modern world. My inspiration for the term came from Marx's observation that a "spectre" was haunting Europe. The idea of a ghost is an apt metaphor for how I perceive the timelessness of these processes within post-Columbian history. The way each process is applied, presented, memorialized, and perceived may change over time (and transformations through time constitute an important line of inquiry in modern-world archaeology), but each process remains remarkably tenacious in structure and application.

For example, the ways in which those in power racialize individuals and groups have changed dramatically over the past five centuries, and the meaning of "race" continues to be transformed by time. Even so, the basic structure of the racialization process—as a hierarchy-imposing structure of superiority/inferiority from above—stubbornly remains intact. The same is true of colonialism. The struggles people face today are often rooted in past colonial malpractice. The staying power of the haunts makes them legitimate subjects for historical archaeology, and it is this quality that transforms them into a central concern of modern-world archaeology.

I also intend the term in a more practical way. I mean to suggest that each haunt hovers over the contemporary practice of archaeology regardless of whether every individual archaeologist acknowledges them. Most traditional historical archaeology is conservative in orientation, with many historical archaeologists tacitly upholding the status quo in their writings, teachings, and practices. Because each haunt floats in the background of all archaeological research, often as an unrecognized presence, my original observation in the *Modern World* book is still relevant.

All of them haunt historical archaeology, trailing the field like four quiet shadows. They exist at every site, on every laboratory table, within every map and chart made. Sometimes one is pushed to the forefront to be the subject of analysis. At other times, they all may hang back like ghostwriters, ever present but unacknowledged and unnamed. Regardless, each subject pervades historical archaeology and so must be acknowledged, understood, and challenged. (1996, p. 57)

Thus historical archaeologists who propose that the haunts are unimportant, either to post-Columbian history or the contemporary practice of archaeology, are ignoring a great deal about recent history. Just like our most immediate ancestors, every archaeologist is equally enmeshed within the haunts' webs. Even archaeologists with privileged backgrounds and unshakably secure positions at elite universities cannot escape them. The most they can do is pretend that the haunts do not exist or that Western societies have "moved beyond them." That each individual and every social group has had different experiences with each haunt does not decrease their significance or mean that they have disappeared. Quite the contrary, the effort to make them disappear—even within the privileged world of professional archaeology—demonstrates their relevance, perhaps as nothing else could. Silencing the uncomfortable has always been a useful tool of the powerful and archaeology is no different in this regard. An example will illustrate the connection between the practice of archaeology and the haunts.

A Brief Example

It would be virtually impossible to conduct archaeological research without capitalism. In fact, the professionalization of archaeology—or at least the regular practice of it that began during the Renaissance—would have been unthinkable without the leisure time afforded to certain members of the upper class. Countless cooks, farmers, herders, bailiffs, and others toiled so that privileged members of capitalist societies had the leisure time to devote to the study of ancient ruins and standing stones. This army of unknown laborers thus made it possible for the discipline to march forward. Thomas Jefferson could never have developed his concepts about American Indian history without ordering his enslaved workers to conduct his excavations. The myth of the Moundbuilders would have taken much longer to discredit without the grunt work of people who were purposefully kept uneducated and oppressed. Heinrich Schliemann was only able to devote his time to searching for Troy because he had made a fortune in the silver business. Without his riches he would have been just another Victorian who had been forced at school to read about the Homeric heroes.

Capitalism undeniably sustains archaeology today. As Dorothy Lippert observed, "[L]ike medieval alchemists, archaeologists have taken base material, the everyday relics of individual lives, and transformed it into a scholarly commodity" (2006, p. 432). This act of commoditization is deeply rooted within capitalism. The capitalist transformation of archaeology has become impossible to ignore because by the late twentieth century more professional archaeologists were employed in private businesses dedicated to cultural resource assessment than by educational institutions (see Chapter 7). The passage of cultural preservation laws throughout the world has transformed much archaeological research into something akin to civil engineering. Like practicing engineers, nonacademic archaeologists consult with government agencies, corporations, and municipalities rather than with students eager to learn. Their "sponsored research" is transformed into a proprietary product to be consumed only by those who have paid for it.

The only thing missing from my analogy with civil engineering is the licensing requirements that ensure the highest standards of practice among engineers. Today almost anyone can claim to be an archaeologist (especially on television and the Internet). The lofty goals of a liberal education, optimistically implemented to create a better world composed of compassionate, knowledgeable citizens, have been replaced with increased service to capitalist expansion. This reality does not disappear simply because some traditionalist archaeologists refuse to acknowledge it.

The connection between archaeology (its practice and how it transforms its basic source material) and capitalism provides but one example of how the haunts of modernity affect daily life. So what's the problem? Why are the haunts controversial?

Criticism comes largely from scholars who have adopted some form of postmodernist thinking. They have taught us that we should be wary of overarching ideas like the haunts because they constitute "meta-narratives." Such scholars state with conviction that meta-narratives are to be avoided at all costs because such strategies of perception force us to see the world through particular lenses. Ardent adherents thus would have us accept that capitalism consists of unrelated practices and actions, that the various expressions of capitalist practice are locally unique. The distinctiveness of the locally relevant means that such practices cannot exert influence over large numbers of people. The idea that many "capitalisms" exist plays into this misunderstanding and dilutes the global affects of capitalism. Many scholars who have accepted some of postmodernism's central tenets seek to make capitalism invisible or to treat it as something entirely natural within the human story.

Modern-world archaeology overtly rejects such thinking and labels it antithetical to the responsible practice of archaeology. For modern-world archaeologists it remains undeniably true that understanding meta-narratives, specifically the four haunts (which I prefer to call "meta-processes"), is essential to conceptualizing the past five centuries—the time in world history when powerful individuals, social groups, and corporations advanced the causes of colonialism, capitalism, Eurocentrism, and racialization. Studying the union of the haunts after about 1500 and continuing ever since is the basic, ultimate, and avowed subject of modern-world archaeology.

The rejection of overarching theories negates the use of the horizontal and vertical models of network theory (see Chapter 3). For such thinkers long-distance impacts cannot be felt because the only influences that can affect people are local and immediate, and the presence of structures through time is impossible to imagine (see Chapter 4). For them capitalism as a meta-narrative of the post-1500 world cannot persist through time, because to conceive it thus would mean that they have accepted it as an overarching process that has molded practice through time.

One last thing about the haunts is important to emphasize. What truly distinguishes the modern world—and what makes it unique in history—is the purposeful combination of the four haunts into a unified (albeit infinitely complex) system of activity, practice, and procedure after about 1500. The precise characteristics concerning the ways in which features of the haunts are expressed, put into practice, or promoted through ideology have been modified throughout modern history—even though their central tenets remain remarkably consistent throughout. The dual nature of the haunts, with equal parts mutability and stability, provides an important concept for the practice of modern-world archaeology.

COLONIALISM

Colonization refers to the spatial movement of people from one cultural region into another's territory with the intent of creating temporary, intermittent, or permanent settlements. In 1849 Edward Gibbon Wakefield, in his *A View of the Art of Colonization*, entrenched this definition in our lexicon once and for all. Wakefield, who was a major proponent of Australian colonization, stressed that it is simply the repositioning of people from one locale to another.

Colonialism, however, has a much more relational meaning and one that is thus significant to modern-world archaeology. By colonialism we refer to the power relations accompanying post-Columbian colonization, rather than simply to the movement of people from one place to another. Colonialism thus establishes a colonizer : colonized social relation that must be understood from the start. Modern-world archaeology is interested in examining the processes of post-Columbian colonialism rather than in attempting to demonstrate the apparent timelessness of colonization throughout human history. Modern-world archaeology adopts an interest in colonialism over colonization because the enforced inequalities of colonialism are much more relevant to the recent (and ongoing) history of the world than are ancient episodes of colonization. Modern-world archaeology is especially interested in investigating the unequal power relations that have been expressed as a result of post-Columbian colonialism. Colonialism is an obvious subject for modern-world archaeology because its historical practice is inexorably linked to the other haunts.

By the start of the nineteenth century, the rulers of small countries in Western Europe—which comprise only a tiny portion of the world's land surface—controlled massive territories and asserted countless rights of conquest over hundreds of millions of colonial "subjects." The desires of European (and later American) rulers to transplant their citizens around the globe—based on diverse political, religious, philosophical, and economic rationales—was a constituent element of the colonialist project, which at its root represents the theory and practice of domination. By the start of the twentieth century, Europe's role in colonizing, conquering, and reshaping had created acute cultural crises in what came to be called the Third World. Colonialism was never merely a natural process that simply happened. Its agents consciously designed its goals and carefully defined its practices.

Social observers living during the age of mercantilism, scribes who directly observed the practices as they occurred, were cognizant of the inequalities inherent in the process. As early as 1542, for instance, Bartolomé de Las Casas highlighted the "atrocities" of the Spanish forces in the New World. Writing in 1612, Sir John Davies—the attorney general of Ireland—noted that "a barbarous Country must be first broken by warre, before it will be capeable [sic] of good Government" (1747 [1612], p. 9). In pondering the question of what constitutes a just war, John Locke observed in the late seventeenth century that conquerors, "usually by . . . force," compel those whom they conquer "with a sword at their breasts, to stoop to his conditions, and submit to such a government as he pleases to afford" those who are conquered (1980 [1690]), p. 97).

By the late eighteenth century, as European colonies spread throughout the world, a number of scholars took notice of the inequalities inherent in the practice of colonialism. Writing in the late eighteenth century, Adam Smith decried the effects that colonialism had on native peoples throughout the colonial world and said that mercantilism is "carried on for the benefit of the rich and the powerful" (1999 [1776], Vol. II, p. 229). Throughout the eighteenth and nineteenth centuries (and even into the early part of the twentieth century), a number of observers reported that colonialism has always been associated with cultural misunderstanding, displacement, violence, and murder.

Modern-world archaeology studies the connections among the haunts, and an important line of investigation concerns the linkage between the European post-Columbian market society and colonialism (and later imperialism). In *Capital* Marx made the connection explicit in his comments about the earliest years of mercantile capitalism. While noting that "plundering, piracy, kidnapping slaves, and colonial conquest" had a long history stretching back into the classical world, he held a special place for the development of merchant capital, which "when it holds a position of dominance, stands everywhere for a system of robbery" (1967 [1867], Vol. III, p. 331).

Marx's reasoning is complex but his argument hinged on the distinctions between different kinds of value (see Chapter 6). In short, Marx argued that trade between a profit-seeking merchant and someone who does not understand or accept the profit motive is unequal because the non-capitalist views the products of his or her labor as having value only in terms of their use. The non-capitalist makes clay pots and shell necklaces to use and trade rather than to sell for profit. The merchant trader, however, takes these objects and after purchasing them thinks about how he might resell them for a greater amount than he originally paid for them. The merchant has taken something intended for use and has converted it into something for sale. This is the robbery Marx wrote about because the profit enriches the merchant at the expense of the producer.

In colonialism combined with mercantilism, the strength of merchant empires depended on "extra-economic" factors—elements that gave an unfair advantage in trade. For example, the seventeenth century Dutch were able to create a huge economic empire because of their command of important shipping routes, their monopoly of certain trading privileges with indigenous potentates, and the sophistication of their financial practices and organizations. Other merchant empires resorted to physical violence and some used varying degrees of coercion and co-optation.

THE CAPITALIST PROJECT

The economic system known as capitalism pervades most of what Western peoples (and increasingly non-Western peoples) do on a daily basis. Capitalism and mercantilism—its progenitor—have impacted peoples' daily lives in myriad ways over the past five centuries. Scholars disagree about the starting date of the capitalist system, but its roots certainly existed in sixteenth century mercantilism when the Dutch East India Company, founded in Amsterdam in 1602, became the world's first multinational corporation.

Most of us tend to think of capitalism as purely an economic system and at its heart it is just this. Upon more careful reflection, however, we must also conclude that the capitalist encourages and enforces social elements that cannot be easily divorced from economics. For this reason the term "capitalist project" more than simply "capitalism" best expresses both the economic and social elements of what at first may appear to be merely a system of market exchange. The idea of the capitalist project also provides a way to understand that mercantilism was an integral part of the process. The capitalist project can be best perceived as economic and "extra-economic" because its impacts extend well beyond the marketplace. The term "capitalist culture" used by many historical archaeologists is inadequate because this label naturalizes the economics and mystifies the practices of capitalist agents. Raising capitalism to the level of culture bestows far too much credit upon it.

The exchange of goods and services for some form of equally exchangeable goods and services has existed for centuries, and archaeologists of ancient civilizations have done much to increase our knowledge about these situations. But an important distinction between ancient and post-1500 systems of trade is the global disruption that characterizes the modern era. Ancient history saw the rise of societies with markets, but the modern era witnessed the rise of the market society. The social relations established between people in a market society are embedded in the economy rather than the other way around. For many the development of these societies threatened humanity's psychological and moral foundations because they undermined long-standing cultural institutions. In other words, they placed the economy above the cultural norms of the society, challenging the idea that the economy should be embedded within social relations.

What makes the market society so unique in human history, and thus why it demands serious archaeological analysis, is the market dependence it commands. Simply put, the market comes between social relations because individuals must enter the marketplace—that is, buy (or create consumer : seller relations)—in order to survive. Living in a market society means having to rely on the market.

Another important distinctive feature of the capitalist project is that within a market society most individuals can gain access to the market by selling the only commodity they truly possess: their ability to work. As Marx noted in *Capital*, the "original sin" of the working class is that "despite all its labour, [it] has . . . nothing to sell but itself" (1967 [1867], Vol. I, p. 713). The basis of the capitalist system is that it separates laborers from everything but their labor, which they are "free" to sell for wages. One of the differences between actual slavery and wage slavery is that laborers give up their freedom willingly in the latter. Individuals owning the means of production need not coerce them to work. If non-owners want to survive, they must surrender their labor power to individuals and corporations who can afford to trade wages for work.

As seen in Chapter 3, capitalism thus creates a distinctive set of relations that can be modeled as networks (human : human and human : nature). Scholars have long debated precisely when and actually how these new relations first appeared. Marx believed that capitalism began in the sixteenth century, even though some elements had appeared in the fifteenth and even in the fourteenth centuries. Others place the development of capitalism in sixteenth century Ireland as a result of England's imposition of colonialism. The often-vicious academic arguments that developed over identifying the first incidence of capitalism, generally termed the "transition debate," continue today.

The transition debate raises an interesting problem for modern-world archaeology. If modern-world archaeologists are explicitly interested in the capitalist project, does this mean they must be blind to much else that has occurred in the world? Do modern-world archaeologists ignore all societies that are not market societies?

Mercantilism and Capitalism

These are important questions but we must remember that capitalism did not spring from thin air. Long before, there existed what Marx referred to as "the pre-historic stage of capitalism." For historical archaeologists this "prehistory" can easily translate into mercantilism, the strategy employed by all those European precapitalist extractors of gold, silver, furs, and humans from outside Europe. Marx believed that the "Monetary (Mercantile) System" represented the historical bridge between the dissolution of the landed estates of feudalism (the serf : lord social relation) and the institution of industrial capitalism (the worker : owner social relation). For him the mercantile system was the first step in the modern system of production.

In the late eighteenth century, Adam Smith outlined the two major benefits a mercantile nation experiences because of foreign trade: it provides a destination for the surplus commodities that cannot be sold at home, and it returns commodities for which demand exists (also see Chapter 6). As mercantilist nations the European superpowers of the sixteenth, seventeenth, and eighteenth centuries realized that the Americas could provide new and seemingly inexhaustible extractive sites for raw materials that could make their nations—and a few select individuals, families, and guilds—immeasurably rich and powerful. The root of mercantile strength, however, rested on a nation's internal qualities. Smith said that mercantile success would come to those countries that exported more goods than they imported (a refrain we still regularly hear today).

The mercantilist process may appear straightforward and commonsensical, and Smith believed that the development of mercantlism and capitalism was entirely natural to the course of human development. Marx, however, provided a more trenchant analysis of the process. As he saw it, mercantilism made it possible to split the exchange process into purchase and sale, such that it was possible to buy without selling (to create a stockpile of commodities) and to sell without buying (to create a stockpile of money). This separation meant that some individuals could exploit the division and thus establish themselves as wealthy—and therefore powerful—elites. These elites, being hard-working merchants of nonroyal birth, could even become richer than the most secure king or queen. Riches could circumvent the perquisites of the nobility in the process of creating a new social hierarchy. As Smith observed, "It is the industry which is carried on for the benefit of the rich and the powerful that is principally encouraged by our mercantile system. That which is carried on for the benefit of the poor and the indigent is too often either neglected or oppressed" (1999 [1776], p. 229). Unfortunately, his sentiment remains relevant today.

The linguistic root of "capitalism" is "capital." Many people equate this term with currency but the term can also refer to tools, machinery, fields, mills, factories, and everything else that might be necessary for production. Sociologist Pierre Bourdieu expanded the meaning of capital to include other forms of amassed wealth. In addition to economic capital (where a person converts his or her time, energy, and strength into income or wages through work), the other forms of capital are "cultural" (e.g., education, knowledge about art and music), "social" (e.g., influential friends and acquaintances in social networks), and "symbolic" (e.g., having a donor's name inscribed on a hospital wall). Each of the different kinds of capital employs currency as a metaphor because an individual or social group can store up "funds" for later use just as if it were a bank account. Cultural capital in the form of a degree from an elite university operates in this manner. Archaeologists who have had the social advantage of obtaining an advanced degree from an elite university do not necessarily have the same challenges as those who did not have the opportunity to enter those ivy-covered halls.

No form of capital can exist outside a social relation. Money mediates between the consumer : seller relation just as wages mediate between the laborer : owner relation. Without the social relation that accompanies it, for example, the U.S. dollar would simply be a rather ugly piece of paper with a number printed on it.

Many historical archaeologists are today engaged in the examination of capitalism and mercantilism. The contributions they may make to our understanding of the material dimensions of the capitalist project are many and varied. On a basic level, by charting the global movement of commoditized artifacts within both capitalist market societies and precapitalist societies with markets, archaeologists can demonstrate the rate at which commodities were spread and identify the social relations they encumbered. The worldwide spread of tea again provides a useful example for many reasons, not the least of which is that its presence in the world spans the mercantile/capitalist divide.

Noncapitalist societies in Asia originally grew tea. With the advent of seventeenth century European mercantilism, tea became a commodity that could be traded worldwide along with its close companion, Chinese export porcelain. For wealthy elites porcelain made in China quickly became the measure of great wealth and exquisite living. In 1724 Daniel Defoe attributed the initial lust for Chinese porcelain to Queen Mary, who had the custom of stuffing the royal palaces with imported vessels. Royal hangers-on and sycophants hoped to amass positions and favors by imitating the queen's behavior.

By the early eighteenth century, the interest in tea and porcelain had trickled down to the masses and high demand by all social classes transformed the production of tea into a plantation staple. It also helped foster the creation of the European ceramics industry (see Chapter 7). The mass production of ceramics made to resemble Chinese export porcelain became a staple within England's manufacturing sector. Armed with the "proper" accouterments, European elites developed a set of manners that were inexorably linked to the refined consumption of tea.

Globalization

Tea and porcelain demonstrate the growing importance of worldwide trade and global marketing over the past few centuries, beginning with European-style mercantilism. By excavating settlements around the world, modern-world archaeologists can tangibly demonstrate the early spread of globalized products and simultaneously illustrate the myriad ways in which local consumers modified the contexts, uses, and meanings of the commodities they acquired.

The inherent historical complexity of capitalist-based globalism means that a universal model of the process is impossible to formulate. A useful line of inquiry, however, involves two interlinked processes: glocalization and grobalization. The terms are cumbersome but the processes they describe are central to understanding the capitalist project. Dialectical thinking helps us appreciate how these two processes are inexorably linked vertically (through time) and horizontally (across space).

Historical archaeologists have long been acquainted with glocalization, or the mixing of the local and the global in ways that create unique cultural expressions throughout the world. Anthropologists once viewed material transformations as examples of acculturation, but today they interpret change as cultural hybridization or creolization. Acculturation tends to be a one-way process, where one culture adopts the practices or material culture of another culture. Hybridization and creolization are two-way processes, where both cultures in contact adopt certain cultural attributes from one another.

Archaeologists interested in globalization must also recognize glocalization because the failure to do so obfuscates, marginalizes, and silences the local practices of indigenous creators and adaptors. In other words, the failure to think along many dimensions at once bestows far too much credit on only one of the entities in contact. For a long time, many scholars viewed native peoples as eager to accept European cultural elements at the expense of their own traditions. Few people today still accept the one-way transfer of culture.

As important as it is, glocalization describes only one side of the globalism process; it creates unrealistic, asymmetric models. This obtains because a complementary process, termed "grobalization," also exists. As explained by George Ritzer, grobalization—the linguistic root refers to capitalism's inherent need to expand or grow—is defined as "the imperialistic ambitions of nations, corporations, organizations, and the like, and their desire and need to impose themselves on various geographic areas" (2003, p. 192). Natives living in eastern North America could not have cut up whole brass kettles to make arrow points and cone-shaped ornaments (an example of glocalization) without the constant influx of whole kettles into their villages and hunting camps (a facet of grobalization).

Glocalization and grobalization thus constitute the dialectical subprocesses that are consciously pursued within globalization. When united they represent the union of opposites, one of the central relations studied in dialectical research. A dialectical understanding is imperative to appreciate their co-occurrence (see Chapter 3). Concentrating solely on glocalization relieves the agents of grobalization of their responsibilities, whereas too strong an emphasis on the agents of grobalization erases the power of indigenous peoples to reject, refine, and modify. When viewed dialectically, glocalization and grobalization define the process of globalism. The production, spread, and mimicry of Chinese export porcelain that began in the seventeenth century illustrates the dialectical nature of globalism and identifies how Europeans learned from Asia to create their own globalized products (though seldom giving credit to their benefactors).

The grobalization/glocalization dialectic is especially pertinent to modern-world archaeology because it references objects, spaces, and peoples. Individual communities, faced with a flood of foreign commodities (see Chapter 6), directly experience the conflicts between the grobal (as advanced by entrepreneurs and their agents) and the glocal (as pursued by local individuals attempting to maintain tradition and manage change in the face of societal transition). The profit motive exhibited by the agents of grobalism seeks to overwhelm local culture because corporations and other market-based institutions must constantly grow if they are to create homogenous lifestyles based on consumerism. Anthropologists witness and experience this struggle when they observe glocalization in action.

The counterpoint is the struggle men and women face when they seek to resist the spread, power, and alleged common sense of mercantilism and capitalism. But globalization never attains homogenization. Within the dominant capitalist nations are a tiny minority of dominating individuals who jealously guard their possessions, wealth, and privilege against the gains of the majority. That glocalization keeps total homogenization from occurring neither lessens the corporate urge to grow nor reduces the power of the modern ideology of consumerism to impel consumers to buy. Witness tea and porcelain.

EUROCENTRISM

At its most basic, Eurocentrism is a form of ethnocentrism that creates the perception that Europe constitutes the center of the universe. As an intellectual concept, it imbues a biased sense of cultural superiority to European peoples who are led to believe that they have intellectual and creative talents that far outstrip those of non-Europeans.

Early anthropology had an important role to play in the development of Eurocentrism because educated elites during the Renaissance, reading the available tracts of primitive ethnography, generally accepted that the traditions and customs of non-Europeans reflected savagery and sacrilege. The most renowned polemists during the age advised that European peoples were specially endowed to conquer the world as part of a universalist, proto-evolutionary doctrine. This view was perfectly consistent with the rationality that characterized the European Enlightenment and, when perverted, led to the eventual development of Social Darwinism. Eurocentrism thus developed as a rather incoherent—albeit generally consistent—set of distorted social theories that have subjugated indigenous ways of being and knowing. The persistence of these social theories has often meant that historical knowledge has been defined in European terms.

Eurocentrism thus has two characteristics of which modern-world archaeologists are aware. First, it is an intellectual perspective some individuals use to perpetuate the centrality of Europe (and the United States) as the pinnacle of human social creation. The general public is most familiar with this sense of the term. One of its practical implications is that it allows politicians, pundits, and nationalist boosters to promote European and American exceptionalism in the present and European exceptionalism in the past. Activists and scholars who believe in social justice and equality struggle against this slanted view of cultural equality.

The second sense of Eurocentrism is best described as the actual practices of the more abstract intellectual perspective. Rather than simply prejudicing scholarship, practical Eurocentrism affects social practices by establishing unequal relationships. Its tenets function in living society and have tangible outcomes when advanced by powerful individuals as practices and legislation. A historian writing a book promoting English exceptionalism as an inborn national trait endowed by providence is guilty of the first sense of Eurocentrism; a British colonial administrator enforcing harsh legal restrictions during the Raj is guilty of the second. The second sense recognizes that Eurocentrism, in addition to being a biased perspective to be shunned in research, demands historical analysis because of its impacts on both natives and newcomers in colonialist environments.

Interestingly, Eurocentrism as a feature of past practice (the second sense) has never been a major topic within historical archaeology even though most contemporary archaeologists have decried the bias of an overt

Eurocentric perspective (the first sense). The historical archaeologists' general neglect of practical Eurocentrism and its real-world impacts represents a significant disciplinary failure. Modern-world archaeology seeks to correct this oversight by explicitly promoting the analysis of Eurocentrism as a historically relevant set of principles, ideas, and practices.

Widespread critical consciousness about the first sense of Eurocentrism surfaced during the rise of multiculturalism, as community activists, cultural survivalists, and politically engaged scholars began to stress that non-Western cultures—including their traditions of art, literature, architecture, dance, and music—have intrinsic value and deserve to be acknowledged on their own terms. Long before the academic "discovery" of Eurocentrism, however, a number of oppressed groups in colonial and postcolonial territories had voiced their opposition to the concept that the world revolved solely around Europe and Europeans. Activities around the world since the 1920s have established coteries of resistance to European imperialism and its associated Eurocentrism.

The European, post-Columbian belief in itself, which in history included the coalescence of the four haunts, constructed Europe as uniquely progressive and innovative. For those who believed, Europe became the quintessential embodiment of cultural exceptionalism. Everyone else in the world was far less creative, moral, and just.

Historians have been especially sensitive to the charge of European exceptionalism, and many of them have exposed the history of the exceptionalist discourse and explicitly disavowed its practice. Other historians have written global histories from a non-Eurocentric perspective. Perhaps the strongest, most concerted effort to demolish the fallacy of Eurocentrism has come from Sinologists. Their examination of global history has demonstrated that many of the cultural features generally attributed to Europe(ans) were actually first developed in Asia, most notably in China. These historians offer a global perspective on modern history that is inclusive without being Eurocentric. They argue against constructing Europe as the world's best and brightest, as they write cross-cultural histories that include—but do not exalt—Europe(ans).

It would be a mistake to imagine that Eurocentrism was practiced outside the ideological bounds of mercantilism and capitalism, because these haunts were deeply interlinked. Without the power of the capitalist project, Eurocentrism would have been much less pervasive; it would have been just another form of ethnocentrism. This fact was not lost on many people, including popular authors. For example, in his thinly veiled autobiography *Burmese Days*, writer George Orwell has one of his characters living in British-controlled Burma say, "Why, of course, the lie [is] that we're here to uplift our poor black brothers instead of to rob them. . . . The British Empire is simply a device for giving trade monopolies to the English" (1934, p. 39). This quote, with its message linking market economics and Eurocentrism, also succinctly establishes the case for racialization.

RACIALIZATION

Racialization is the process of inventing biological and social inferiority using ideology, pseudo-science, administrative power, repressive authority, and other legal and extra-legal forms of domination and oppression. Racialization is an especially pernicious form of social control because it relegates whole groups of people to inferior social positions based on some perceived characteristic—which may include skin color, facial features, religion, customs, language, traditions, and even dress. The practical outcome of this process is that people identified as exhibiting the key characteristics are collectively grouped into a specific "race." Used in this manner, race is different from ethnicity because racial identification comes from the outside rather than the inside (as is the case for ethnic affiliation). Racialization is pernicious and hurtful, whereas ethnic identification is neither.

As a process racialization is mutable over time, such that the practices of one era may not be relevant in another. At certain times and in some places, individuals promoting a particular definition of race can base their understanding on such complex notions as lineage, physical type, social position, and class. A social practice like racial intermarriage, for example, may be acceptable in one generation and outlawed in the next. The promoters of a particular racialized view can present their ideas within a nation's dominant discourse using meanings that are dependent upon historical circumstance. Racialization can also be used as an element of a broader political project.

A key element of racialization, however, is that it establishes a social hierarchy such that those who are judged to be at the top of the racial order are generally the same people who enforce the hierarchy, while those at the bottom tend to be groups with little social power. In the early nineteenth century, Samuel Morton observed in 1839 that the "Caucasian race" is distinguished by the highest intellectual endowments; Chinese, on the other hand are ingenious and imitative but insincere and jealous. As an educated member of American society, Morton felt confident that he could make such outrageous claims and have their meaning perfectly understood by his readers, who were also elite members of the racialized hierarchy.

In the United States, the attempted destruction of the indigenous cultures and the subsequent importation of enslaved men and women of African descent have meant that racial assignment has always been an integral part of American history. The long history of racial classification, however, has not made race an easily examined subject. The nature of racial assignment is dynamic, meaning that the concept of what constitutes a race is free to change at any time. The fluctuating nature of racial concepts in the United States is even expressed in the seemingly rigid world of jurisprudence, where a famous case in Louisiana proved that a person's racial classification can be assigned by court order.

The enforced enslavement of people of color, coupled with the mass influx of European immigrants to the United States in the nineteenth century, created a new and incredibly complex dialogue about racialization. The separation of "colored" people from those deemed "uncolored" led to the invention of the white race. This ordeal is still being experienced at the commencement of the twenty-first century, but Americans were especially challenged during the nineteenth century to ponder their conceptions of race and to rethink the meaning of whiteness. Many of the elites who sat atop the social order and who were educated at Harvard University—a historic site of academic racism—overtly avowed, and often loudly proclaimed, their commitment to the so-called "Anglo-Saxon complex." Advocates of this view, which some termed the "cult of the Anglo-Saxon," maintained that everything desirable derived from the blending of English and Germanic cultures; conversely, everyone and everything not of this heritage was inherently inferior. The nation's wealthiest social, political, and business leaders did not hesitate to promote their Anglo-Saxon heritage in published volumes extolling their collective virtues, wealth, and power. The connection between racial assignment and Eurocentrism amply demonstrates how the haunts can be made to work together within a sociohistorical setting.

In the United Kingdom, the working out of the Anglo-Saxon complex has been described as an inclusiveness that appears muffled. Those cultures on the "Celtic fringe" (Scots, Welsh, Irish) were incorporated into a concept of Britishness that was essentially English rather than multicultural. Muffled inclusiveness is an inherently ideological process, and since the ruling American elite during the nineteenth century generally accepted the notion of Anglo-Saxon greatness, it is no great leap to suppose that they also accepted the English concept of inclusiveness. In the American version of muffled inclusiveness, peoples deemed "lesser" for whatever reason faced the enforced muting of their traditions and customs by the dominant culture. All U.S. citizens are to be Americans first and foremost. The now-standard metaphor of the United States as a tossed salad rather than a melting pot indicates that muffling does not necessarily cause the complete elimination of those cultural elements non-Anglo-Saxon groups cherish the most.

The Anglo-Saxon complex usually incorporates the racial understanding of the dominant capitalist class. The complexity inherent in the incorporation of non-Anglo-Saxon immigrants into a social fabric makes it difficult to generalize. The precise experiences differ depending upon myriad social, historical, political, and economic factors. Even so, the uniqueness to be found in specific historical cases—when viewed on the smallest scale—need not negate the discovery of commonalities when inspected on a broader scale. What might at first appear unique in one place might seem upon closer study to be universal. In other words, constructions like the

Anglo-Saxon complex were not unique to the United States, even though its particular expression in American history may be unique to one sociohistorical moment. Other locales also experienced racial complexes of their own. For example, the Andean natives made to labor in the colonial Spanish wine industry could be not considered victims of the Anglo-Saxon complex, even though they were most certainly racialized.

Racism is an outward manifestation of the racialization process rather than a cognitive defect existing in the minds of a few deviant individuals. Racism is structurally imbued in the social system through the practice of racialization. The dominant ideology of Western, liberal societies proffers that a racist person who lives in what is presented as a tolerant, multiethnic society must be mentally flawed to hold such antisocial beliefs. Nonracists in such societies tend to believe that the acts of violence and discrimination perpetrated in the name of race lie outside the bounds of civil society and justifiably condemn them.

The view that racism is a trait of defective thinking is attractive within the context of a liberal democracy, but the longevity of racialization in history—despite its fluid character, changing expression, and various targets—obviously refutes the psychological explanation of race. The increased acceptance of human diversity, advanced through concerted educational efforts, should have meant that racially motivated hatreds would have disappeared decades ago. If only a few deranged individuals were responsible, then education should have eliminated their hatreds as unreasonable. That this has not happened must mean that race-based hierarchies are a part of many social structures.

THE CONFLUENCE OF THE HAUNTS IN THE MODERN WORLD

The archaeology of the modern world provides for an explicit study of the history of a time when merchant capital and the capitalist project were being consciously linked with the other three haunts to reach around the world and attempt to control it. Rather than shy away from a concept of the "modern," modern-world archaeology seeks to (a) investigate the complex reproduction of modernity throughout the world; (b) embrace the confusion between the local and the global; and (c) celebrate the dissonance between globalized, regionalized, and localized sociohistorical contexts that have been created since about 1500.

No need exists to establish the initial date of the modern era or to decide how to divide it into discrete historical periods. We know, for example, that capitalism in its present form developed at some point during the late eighteenth century, but that mercantilism was its progenitor. Feudalism, a completely different mode of production, existed before mercantilism but also gave birth to it. To propose that modern-world archaeology encompasses the entire sweep of human history would be a case of intellectual overreaching. Rather, the subject matter of modern-world archaeology begins with the confluence and interaction of the forces, ideas, ideologies, creations, and developments of the four haunts (Figure 3). This is the post-Columbian world we inhabit today, a five-hundred-year "historical moment" composed of innumerable other moments that exist within a diverse set of frames. They create horizontal and vertical networks modern-world archaeologists can investigate in countless ways (see Chapter 3).

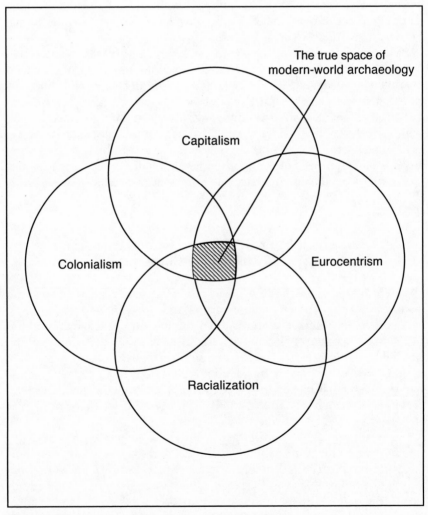

Figure 3. The true space of modern-world archaeology.

Modern-world archaeology accepts that sometime around 1500 a history-altering conjunction of four forces united to create numerous small new worlds and one huge new world. The four forces had (have) coeval planes of existence and in the broadest sense were (are) pan-cultural. Each one was (is) enacted in the post-Columbian world as a complex, multidimensional series of actions, practices, and traditions within structures (see Chapter 5) that are similar—though not identical—in form and design. The execution of these forces, in different ways in disparate places, creates modern history.

The haunts were (and still are) tightly interlinked and coterminous in the post-Columbian world and their intersection is the site of modern-world archaeology's analysis (see Figure 2). The comingling of the haunts, however, does not mean that any single archaeologist should think that he or she must examine them all at once. The complexities and myriad real-world application of the subprocesses within each haunt are so numerous and varied that such a study would be virtually impossible for one person to undertake. Two central points of modern-world archaeology are that an archaeologist claiming to practice it must acknowledge the network relationships that existed in post-1500 history and undertake to investigate at least two of the haunts in the particular context under study. For example, when investigating a single settler settlement in colonial South Africa, the modern-world archaeologist may wish to concentrate on the association between the market society and Eurocentrism.

This broad-scale research does not negate the archaeologist's ability to present a concise, highly detailed description of documentary history or excavated remains. A more traditional historical archaeologist may terminate the research at a single frame, and this is perfectly fine. Modern-world archaeologists, however, would see this research effort—though perhaps extremely useful—as missing an important opportunity to connect the site's residents with myriad other worlds. This is the challenge of modern-world archaeology. It forces historical archaeologists to acknowledge wider worlds and to "think outside the site." We should not be discouraged by the difficulties this research entails.

SUGGESTED READINGS

Colonialism

Césaire, Aimé. 2000. *Discourse on Colonialism*. Translated by Joan Pinkham. Monthly Review Press, New York.
    A classic, and much-cited, overview of the process of colonialism.

Cooper, Frederick and Ann Laura Stoler (editors). 1997. *Tensions of Empire: Colonial Cultures in a Bourgeois World*. University of California Press, Berkeley.

Provides chapters in which the authors investigate the tensions that have existed in the world between colonizers and the colonized.

Las Casas, Bartolomé de. 1992 [1542]. *A Short Account of the Destruction of the Indies*. Edited and translated by Nigel Griffin. Penguin, London.
    The most famous sixteenth century account of the atrocities committed by the Spanish in colonial New Spain. Must reading.

Lippert, Dorothy. 2006. Building a Bridge to Cross a Thousand Years. *American Indian Quarterly* 30:431–440.
    Explores the often-tenuous relationships between archaeology and Native Americans.

Capitalism

Bourdieu, Pierre. 1986. The Forms of Capital. In *Handbook of Theory and Research for the Sociology of Education*, edited by John G. Richardson, pp. 241–258. Greenwood Press, New York.
    A nice introduction to the various forms of capital. One of the author's most concise statements.

Marx, Karl. 1967 [1867]. *Capital: A Critique of Political Economy*. 3 vols. Edited by Frederick Engels. Translated from the Third German Edition by Samuel Moore and Edward Aveling. International Publishers, New York.
    The classic work on capitalism. Challenging reading, but required.

Ritzer, George. 2003. The Globalization of Nothing. *SAIS Review* 23:189–200.
    A short statement about the relationship between capitalism and the globalization process.

Smith, Adam. 1999 [1776]. *The Wealth of Nations*. 2 vols. Edited by Andrew Skinner. Penguin, London.
    Along with Marx's *Capital*, one of the most important investigations of mercantilism and capitalism, but from the perspective of the late eighteenth century.

Wood, Ellen Meiksins. 2002. *The Origin of Capitalism: A Longer View*. Verso, London.
    A brilliant analysis of the creation and development of capitalism.

Eurocentrism

Amin, Samir. 1989. *Eurocentrism*. Translated by Russell Moore. Monthly Review Press, New York.

An important investigation into the meaning of Eurocentrism as a special kind of ethnocentrism.

Orser, Charles E. Jr. 2012. An Archaeology of Eurocentrism. *American Antiquity* 77:737–755.
My statement on the importance of using archaeology to understand Eurocentrism and its importance to modern-world archaeology.

Orwell, George. 1934. *Burmese Days*. Harper & Brothers, New York.
An enlightening look, in novel form, at the realities of Eurocentrism and colonialism.

Prashad, Vijay. 2007. *The Darker Nations: A People's History of the Third World*. New Press, New York.
An excellent account of the Third World's role in world history.

Racialization

Allen, Theodore W. 1997. *The Invention of the White Race*. 2 vols. Verso, London.
An important study of how whiteness came about in the modern world.

Fredrickson, George M. 2002. *Racism: A Short History*. Princeton University Press, Princeton, NJ.
A key study of race and racism. Short and readable.

Miles, Robert. 1989. *Racism*. Routledge, London.
The book for learning about the concept of racialization as a process in the post-Columbian world.

Orser, Charles E. Jr. 2004. *Race and Practice in Archaeological Interpretation*. University of Pennsylvania Press, Philadelphia.
Orser, Charles E., Jr. 2007. *The Archaeology of Race and Racialization in Historic America*. University Press of Florida, Gainesville.
Two books that present my in-depth analyses of race and racialization in historical archaeology. The books mentioned throughout this primer.

STUDY QUESTIONS

1. How does colonialism differ from colonization? Find an example of each in the archaeological literature.

2. Describe a recent situation in which you have taken part in the capitalist project.

3. Think of a historically known indigenous culture and list your own examples of how Eurocentrism has affected it during and after its initial contact with Europeans.

4. Give three examples of how racialization might have affected the culture you identified in #3 above.

CHAPTER 3

THE FOUNDATION

Four basic perspectives for investigating the past are central to modern-world archaeology. I adapt these perspectives from the works of various scholars who practice outside archaeology, for none of their ideas were developed specifically with archaeological analysis in mind. As a result one of the primary tasks of modern-world archaeology is to mold them to the realities of archaeological research. Each perspective can be applied perfectly well on its own, but I combine them in modern-world archaeology because I believe that their linkage provides insightful ways to gather data, assess evidence, and frame interpretations. The four perspectives, when combined, empower archaeologists who investigate the most recent five centuries to conduct archaeological studies that are relevant to present-day lived experience, while at the same time retaining the commitment to serious archaeological scholarship.

The four overarching perspectives are structural history, network theory, world-systems analysis, and dialectical thinking. These provide the foundation for modern-world archaeology. Each one makes a specific contribution to the construction of modern-world archaeology, but they only attain their true interpretive power in archaeology when used together. My presentation of each as independent—as they were originally proposed—is simply a convention required by the realities of explanation. Taken individually, structural history, network theory, world-systems analysis, and dialectics have generated a considerable body of literature completely divorced from archaeological thought. I seek to demonstrate throughout this primer how ideas and concepts from each can, and indeed must, be applied in modern-world archaeology.

STRUCTURAL HISTORY

The significance of structural history begins with historian Fernand Braudel's model of historical time and extends outward from there.

Braudel's concepts, if not their exact application, constitute the base-level foundation of modern-world archaeology. His commitment to using different scales of analysis to understand the complex cultural history of the modern world is perfectly suited to the demands of modern-world archaeology.

Braudel presented his ideas on structural history in his magisterial *The Mediterranean and the Mediterranean World in the Age of Philip II*, first published in French in 1949. This two-volume work is arguably the most prominent early work in what is termed the *"Annales* paradigm." This name derives from the journal *Annales d'histoire économique et sociale* (later renamed *Annales, Economies, Sociétés, Civilizations*), published in France by a group of historians who were dissatisfied with traditional historiography. The paradigm of the *Annalists* was the brainchild of Marc Bloch and Lucien Febvre, the historians who first edited the journal. Their ultimate goal was to reorient historical analysis by moving it away from political history and toward social, cultural, and economic history. Their ideas initially took shape prior to the commencement of the Second World War, but their work received its greatest fulfillment after the war with Febvre and his associates' innovative studies of medieval and early modern French history. (Bloch was captured and murdered by the Gestapo in 1944 while a member of the French Resistance.)

The development of the *Annales* school was completely independent of anything that had occurred in American anthropology, but readers familiar with the history of anthropology will recognize that the goal of writing sociocultural history was consistent with the school of American historical anthropology practiced by A. L. Krober, Robert Lowie, and others—although the connection between these two strains of historical analysis was seldom made explicit. The twentieth century segmentation of the academic disciplines served to create an artificial boundary between socioculturally minded historians and historically minded anthropologists, even though the connections between them (in methods and many topics of interest) is obvious. Today any concrete dividing line between sociocultural history and historical anthropology is spurious. Historians regularly investigate non-Western cultures just as anthropologists are widely known to study Western societies. Though clearly trained in the tradition of European history, Braudel understood the wisdom of including—and in fact emphasizing—social and cultural history in his groundbreaking efforts.

Braudel's Model

Braudel organized his history of the Mediterranean during the reign of King Philip II of Spain—who ruled from 1556 to 1598—around a concept of "levels" or "planes" (Figure 4). The ideas behind this framework constitute the foundational underpinnings of modern-world archaeology be-

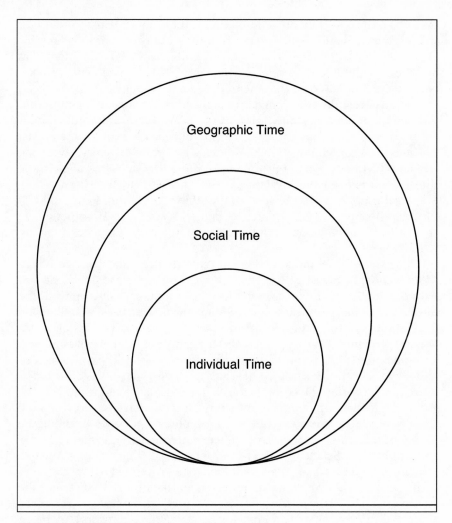

Figure 4. Braudel's "levels" or "planes."

cause his multiscalar model inspires the analytical rigor and philosophical perspective of the field.

Braudel's initial plane was "geographical time." This is history that passes almost imperceptibly. All change on this plane occurs slowly in an ever-reconstituting series of cycles, including human relationships with the environment. Braudel never saw the environment as a mere backdrop for human social action. Rather, he perceived it as an active historical agent and argues that historians should always consider the weather, climate, topography, and other natural features of a region as more than simply a dramatic backdrop for human action. The height of mountains, presence of valleys, strength and flow of rivers, and distribution of flora are tangible features with which humans interact. This understanding is consistent with archaeological thinking since at least the late 1960s, when many archaeologists were influenced by the emerging ecology movement.

Because Braudel envisioned humans as directly engaged with the environment, he dedicates the first part of *The Mediterranean* to the mountains, plains, rivers, boundaries, coasts, and seas as sites where past societies experienced life within large-scale geographical spaces over long stretches of time (thus the prominence of the Mediterranean Sea in the title). Readers even slightly familiar with his work will recognize geographical time as the *longue durée*. It is within this plane of long-term history that he and subsequent archaeologists, historians, and others have sought to illuminate and understand human *mentalités*, or long-lasting worldviews.

Braudel's model moved closer to the individual in Part Two of *The Mediterranean* by investigating "social time." His concern in this plane was with the duality of human structures, so he simultaneously examined the mechanisms that permit the operation of social structures as well as the development of the structures themselves. His research in this plane involved "structure" (the permanent and the slow moving; mechanisms) and "conjuncture" (the ephemeral and the rapid; practices). The contradictory nature of social time means that the analysis of everyday life is difficult because of the constant blending of the changing and the enduring.

To understand the inherent difficulty, Braudel delved deeply into the realities of sixteenth century Mediterranean life by closely examining the slowly transforming structures of daily experience. So, for example, he analyzed physical distances in the region (such as the interactions between settlement structures) and the time it took for a letter to pass from the hand of the writer to the eyes of the intended reader (the interaction between the environmental and the transportation structures). In the same vein, he considers the value of money and precious metals, trade, transport, mobility, poverty, and other subjects situated between the *longue durée* and the most individualistic third plane, "individual time."

Braudel called individual time *l'histoire événementielle* (event history) because it represents the sequence of specific happenings. This plane is familiar ground for most historians, including those who are interested in society. Braudel presented this time as rapid, brief, and nervous. Its rich human content makes it the most exciting plane. But this plane is also the most dangerous one; it is here that historians do their most difficult work of reading and evaluating the thoughts, feelings, and expressed beliefs of the chroniclers of the past. Historians coming from the vantage point of their own time must be extremely sensitive to two sets of biases, prejudices, and individual perspectives: those contained within the written documents they examine (past) and those they themselves hold (present). Historians have been concerned with objectivity for many years and Braudel's comments merely substantiated the significance of constantly being reflective during the research process. In Part Three, then, Braudel worked on the individual plane to write the history of the Mediterranean using the actions of individuals in war and peace and in glory and ignominy. What is special in his presentation, however, is that he established the loci of individual time by having already investigated social and geographical time. Braudel fully contextualized individual time in a manner entirely familiar to archaeologists, including all historical archaeologists investigating an individual site in minute detail.

Braudel's study of the Mediterranean world is widely viewed as one of the greatest historical works of the twentieth century. His research, detailed and sweeping at the same time, suggested a new direction for historical analysis and inspired generations of historians. His works have impacted archaeological theory in ways he probably would never have imagined.

Braudel and the Modern World

Shortly after the French publication of *The Mediterranean*, Febvre—to whom Braudel had dedicated the book—asked him to write a volume on the economic history of pre-industrial Europe for Febvre's new series entitled *World Destinies (Destins du Monde)*. Braudel agreed to his mentor's request, knowing that he would have to expand his range beyond the Mediterranean and include a broader length of time. He originally viewed his task as writing merely an overview summarizing the works of other historians, but as he began the research he quickly realized that the economic conditions in pre-industrial Europe were much more complicated than previous economic historians had portrayed. His response is completely understandable given that he had broken the historical mold with his Mediterranean study, and having had the experience of writing multiscalar history, he was undoubtedly hesitant to abandon his new model.

The results of Febvre's confidence in Braudel were *Capitalism and Material Life, 1400–1800* (first published in French in 1967) and a three-volume expansion entitled *Civilization and Capitalism: 15th-18th Century* (first published in French in 1979). The first book was slightly revised and republished as Volume I of the second book with the new subtitle *The Structures of Everyday Life: The Limits of the Possible*. Braudel's ability to move within and between the different scales of analysis amply demonstrated the interpretive power of his method. In Volume I Braudel provided a splendid model for modern-world archaeology because of his thoughtful mix of specific detail and global breadth.

Given the scale of the task at hand, Braudel devised another tripartite model to help organize his analysis. This model, distinct from although similar to the one he had constructed for *The Mediterranean*, consisted of material life, economic life, and capitalism. In Volume I he focused specifically on material life, a topic most relevant to historical archaeology, including modern-world archaeology. In Volumes II and III, he considered commerce and global capitalism, respectively—topics especially relevant to modern-world archaeology. Here I restrict my exploration to the first volume, because even in this relatively focused work on material culture Braudel could not help but explain its broad connections. It is his ability to understand the many linkages between temporal and spatial scales that makes his work so illustrative for modern-world archaeology.

Braudel's first sentence in Volume I, that "[m]aterial life is made up of people and things," clearly resonates with archaeologists, and this sentence taken by itself may account for the interest many archaeologists have shown in his work. The topics he explored in the volume—food and drink, housing and clothing, and similar topics related to everyday life—are directly relevant to historical and modern-world archaeology. Of particular significance is Braudel's ability to move effortlessly between the tiny and the huge. For example, his exploration of the developments of the European fireplace and stove was perfectly consistent with his broader explanation of the "dietary revolutions of the eighteenth century." In the first case his interest was directed toward the fourteenth century German use of potters' clay to fashion furnaces, while in the second he considered the widely divergent (though entirely relevant) native societies of the eastern United States and Polynesia to explain the inherently global—albeit often unrealized—nature of the modern world.

Braudel was deeply attuned to and totally unapologetic about the central importance he placed on material objects in the creation of everyday life. He linked the development of manners to the use of knives and forks in Germany, he explored the need for clean drinking water and illustrates the design of well-cisterns in Venice, and he linked the transportation of tea from China to the English use of lead- and tin-lined chests—all topics relevant to traditional historical archaeology. Braudel does not shy away from overtly considering material culture as an important historical subject. In fact, he readily acknowledged its central place in human activity. His inclusion of period paintings depicting the use of material objects—white clay smoking pipes, cups for drinking chocolate, and coarse earthenwares—is a technique historical archaeologists have used effectively ever since.

Braudel's Structures

One of the keys to understanding Braudel's contribution to the writing of history—and, by extension, to the practice of modern-world archaeology—stems from his use of the term "structures." Braudel used this term to mean organizations with relatively stable and cohesive sets of relationships that extend through time. He views some of these structures as elements of geographical time (the *longue durée*), as fixed constructs that both hinder and shape history. Other structures appearing in social time (the *moyenne durée*) also affect human history, even though they are more short-term in duration. The environment serves as an active agent, working to direct and guide human activity within the confines of the vagaries of the ecosystem, but the structures still have the ability to constrain humanity (see Chapter 4).

Braudel was unquestionably a historian by training and inclination. Nonetheless, he freely acknowledged the many connections existing between historical interpretation and social science analysis and he encourages the cross-fertilization of ideas, concepts, and methods. Disciplinary conventions and traditions frequently keep anthropologists and historians apart, even though the work of each often overlaps in engaging ways. This is something that Braudel, as a historical pioneer, understood very well.

Braudel's concepts and perspectives about structural history are adopted in the multiscalar vision of modern-world archaeology. Taken at its broadest scale, this vision incorporates a conscious linkage between the specific and the general, the local and the global. Braudel wrote history in such a way that he is able to move between analytical planes with expert precision as he provides a conceptual model for further research. Even if we ignore his broader scheme of writing global history using detailed specifics, we must admire the ways in which he connects the material world with human experience. Any historical archaeologist reading his books for the first time would be challenged to argue for his irrelevance. Many anthropologists have cited his works or have tacitly furthered his goals by demonstrating—in both Western and non-Western settings—that structures of life not only exist, but that they perpetuate inequality through their very presence. Such frameworks create and maintain inequality and the invented inequality supports the framework.

NETWORK THEORY

Braudel modeled social action as occurring within webs or networks of interaction and an understanding of network relations is central to modern-world archaeology. As a result it is necessary to appreciate the basics of network theory because network theorists, principally researchers analyzing social rather than purely physical networks (such as roads and pipelines), have conducted numerous studies that outline the ways in which network theory can be beneficial to the archaeologist's efforts to interpret the modern world.

The idea underlying the use of network theory in modern-world archaeology is that individuals and social groups hold themselves together through a series of complex interrelationships that can be conceptualized as webs. Numerous anthropologists have acknowledged that individuals cannot survive as lone actors in the world and that human existence without social interaction is impossible. Anthropologists who have written about network relations have stressed the multiscalar nature of these connections, starting perhaps with British social anthropologist A. R. Radcliffe-Brown. Radcliffe-Brown, remarking on the importance of networks, said that "[a] particular social relation between two persons . . . exists only as part of a wide network of social relations, involving many other persons" (1940, p. 3). Later anthropologists also stressed the significance of social networks and the necessity to understand these webs of interaction throughout the entirety of human history. Most concluded that human beings need one another to survive, that social relationships constitute the basic stuff of human life.

One of the most important analytical implications of adopting a network perspective is that it frees investigators from evoking the mysteries of Culture (with a capital "C") to explain the past. I have referred to "culturalist interpretations" in earlier writings as those cases in which archaeologists have sought to explain human action solely in terms of culture while ignoring social interaction. Many archaeologists seem to believe that we can explain the past solely in terms of cultural conventions rather than through the creation and enactment of personal interactions created within systems of culture. Modern-world archaeology is impossible without a clear understanding of networks of interaction, and any historical archaeologist who ignores the multidimensional connections that were enacted at any individual historical property is not practicing modern-world archaeology.

Landscape studies in traditional historical archaeology are often rife with culturalist interpretations. For example, traditional historical archaeologists are inclined to invoke the concept of the "cultural landscape" when considering the settlements of immigrants. They largely assume that immigrants attempted to create little pieces of their home culture in a new environment. To some extent this is true; people do tend to perform familiar activities, even—or perhaps especially—when they are in a strange place. They may build their houses using traditional methods and styles and may practice their religion using time-honored rituals. This all makes perfect sense on one level.

When viewed more critically, however, this rather simplistic model can be seen to run directly counter to Braudel's use of the landscape as more than simply a backdrop for human endeavors. Braudel's multiscalar perspective promoted the idea that the environment is an active participant in the activities performed. The settlers in question, for instance, may have built their houses in stone in the home country, but when they learned that their new environment did not have stone worth quarrying, they may have adapted their old techniques to construction with wood. They may even have modeled their dwellings on the indigenous structures they observed around them or used locally available materials to mimic a traditional feature.

A network approach rejects the culturalist argument by proposing instead that landscapes are conscious human creations resulting from the outcomes of a complex set of historically dependent human : human and human : ecosystem relationships. We can term the results "cultural" if we wish, but if our analyses are focused on the social relationships enacted within the networks of interaction—rather than the mysteries of Culture—we stand a much better chance of providing more satisfying interpretations of the past.

Social Network Theory

Network theory has generated a huge body of scholarship, most of which is not relevant to archaeological practice. Much practical research has been conducted on physical networks such as sewer and computer systems. A great deal of network theory, however, involves the analysis of social networks and is termed "social network theory." The goal of using social network theory in archaeology is to devise ways of making this body of research applicable to the realities of archaeological practice. Initial attempts by archaeologists to use social network theory have often concerned the adaptation of geographical models to settlement systems.

At the most basic level, the human : human and human : ecosystem relations noted by Braudel constitute sociohistorical networks. Networks are easy to conceptualize as a drawing of points connected by lines. Formal network theorists refer to the points as "nodes" or "vertices" and the lines as "links" or "edges" (Figure 5). Analysts characterize graphic drawings of networks as "graph diagrams" but use the term "sociogram" to describe social networks.

Networks of interaction exist because individuals and social groups maintain many relationships through time. These relationships can take the form of "vertical" or "horizontal" linkages. Vertical linkages are hierarchical and relate to social units of increasingly larger sizes. Horizontal linkages are enacted within a historical period or cultural setting as contemporaneous connections over various dimensions of space (Figure 6). In the illustration the horizontal linkages occur within the same plane. Such connections might be based on family ties, clan membership, economic relationships, political affiliations, or any other social construction that binds people together. The nodes, therefore, can represent individuals, neighborhoods, political entities, villages, cities, or continents. The links can be cognitive (marriage, kin, membership) and/or physical (streets, roads, rivers).

The vertical linkages extend between planes. They can also be cognitive or physical and rooted in tradition (folklore, religious ritual, custom)

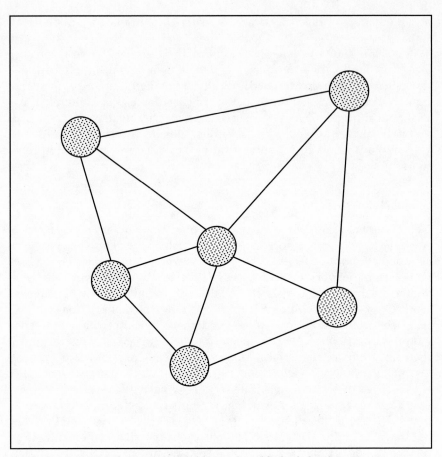

Figure 5. Networks showing nodes (vertices) and links (edges).

or place (being situated in a locale with a specific cultural meaning, such as a sacred mountain or neighborhood). For example, the eighteenth century British trading network that linked India, the West Indies, and London can be conceptualized as a horizontal network because it operated through geographical space during a specific period of history. We can envision the vertical linkages if we move to the frame of the *longue durée* or the *moyenne durée*. A traditional historical archaeologist may wish to identify the actions of the British as representing a cultural tradition (a vertical network connection). But without considering the diverse environments and the myriad cultures with which the traders and merchants came into contact (the horizontal linkages), not to mention the long-term implications of these entanglements, the research would not constitute modern-world archaeology.

Another vertical linkage might be the connection between objects used in a past sociohistorical context and those same objects put on display in a

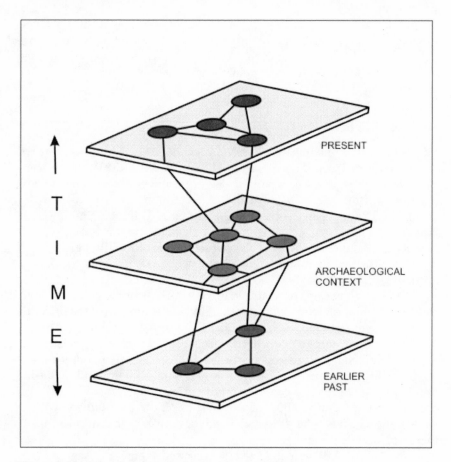

PRESENT

ARCHAEOLOGICAL
CONTEXT

EARLIER
PAST

T
I
M
E

Figure 6. Horizontal and vertical network connections.

museum exhibit. The objects are linked through time, even though the nature of their horizontal linkages have dramatically changed or disappeared altogether. Historical analysis at the narrowest frame is required, even in modern-world archaeology, because new vertical and horizontal linkages can be created and old links can be reshaped at any time. Only the careful study of all extant evidence (historical, archaeological, geographical) can pinpoint their dates of creation, maintenance, and disuse.

The concepts of horizontal and vertical connections are centrally important to the practice of modern-world archaeology. Modern-world archaeologists understand that networks constitute sociospatial units—that the interactions of individuals and groups operate simultaneously in social and spatial contexts. The interactions between the nodes in a network are understood to have occurred within a specific set of relations (human : human and human : environment) rather than within a vaguely imagined cultural landscape. It may be necessary for purposes of analysis, however, to separate the elements of a sociospatial network into its social and spatial components. Such separation is only a research convention and does not mirror lived reality. At some point the analyst must bring them together again.

Social Interaction

Ethnographers, ethnoarchaeologists, and sociologists can witness the ways in which different social groups and individuals (the nodes) interact in social space. Among the Ethiopian Maale, for instance, anthropologist Donald Donham modeled their concept of "working together" as existing within two kinds of networks: blocs and webs. In the bloc model each household works for every other one at some point in time, but in the web model a household may work with another household—although not necessarily with all of them. Both cases, however, are rooted in network connections.

Historians have also been able to use network theory to explore the social relationships of people in the past. In their examination of the fifteenth century power structure created by the Florentine powerbroker Cosimo de' Medici, for example, political scientists John Padgett and Christopher Ansell identified nine types of network relationships that operated among Medici's elite class members. The nature of the connections binding the individuals together was a complex mix of marriage, personal friendship, politics, and economics. The interwoven connections maintained by these aristocratic social climbers created a web of networks that allowed them to dominate their social environment.

Research reveals that the Medicis amassed their inordinately large storehouse of power by being circumspect in forging social connections. The Medicis were more likely than other old-money families to fraternize with the nouveau riche. Their willingness to interact with "new money" elites was a strategy that increased the reach and resilience of their social network. Other Florentine elite families were not as careful. Without their broad network of associates, clients, and presumed friends, however, the Medicis would have been just another wealthy family whose names would have been known to only a few historians of fifteenth century Florence. Today their social network is remembered as a model of how early modern elites gathered and maintained power, authority, and riches.

Unlike anthropologists and sociologists, archaeologists must discover the nature, composition, and extent of network relationships without the assistance or benefit of direct observation. Like historians they must piece together history's social networks from the often fragmentary and incomplete evidence left behind. The presence of written records and other sources of textual and even oral information make network analysis possible in historical archaeology. The presence of maps, plans, and transcribed direct observations expand our knowledge of sociospatial networks often without relying solely on large-scale regional surveys.

One of the great advantages of textual sources for historical archaeology is the often one-to-one correlation they provide between archaeological entities and the documents themselves. A historical archaeologist may have access to a colonial Spanish map made for the site on which excavation is planned. If sufficiently detailed, the map may permit the identification of both spatial and social networks. The power structure operating in a Spanish colonial town in South America might be observable in the design and location of buildings around a central plaza or near a mission site. A plat of the area, even one that is crudely drawn, may provide important clues about the sociospatial networks once in operation there.

All historical archaeologists should know how to evaluate textual sources and appreciate how historically contemporaneous sources, even if inaccurate, can contribute abundant information about past social networks. One question worth pondering, however, is how much training in historiography today's historical archaeologists are actually receiving in their various departments of anthropology. Anecdotal information suggests that the answer is "Not much." If my impression is correct, the failure to teach historical archaeologists the historians' methods and techniques of critical evaluation represents a huge failure of the educational system. One of the main goals of modern-world archaeology is to link social theory and history. Historical archaeologists should receive as much training in historical methods, interpretation, and theory as they normally receive in anthropology courses dedicated to the same subjects.

Network Units of Analysis

Formal network analysis gives initial prominence to people and places as nodes and links. The resultant network analysis can be used to model relationships between individuals, between social groups, between individuals and social groups, between individuals and places, and between social groups and places. Analyses can provide both synchronic and diachronic dimensions separately, but one goal of modern-world archaeology is to offer multiscalar interpretations that are simultaneously synchronic and diachronic.

Several linkages lie at the heart of social network analysis. These connections can be described, in ascending order of size, as:

- Actor.
- Dyad.
- Triad.
- Subgroup.

- Group.
- Social network.

The spatial corollaries of these terms, for archaeological purposes, might be:

- Site.
- Two sites.
- Three sites.
- Area.
- Region.
- Network.

These terms are idealized because more contextualized terms should be substituted for any sociohistorical analysis. For example, a social network might be found to consist of the following levels:

- Individual.
- Nuclear family.
- Extended family.
- Neighborhood.
- Urban network.
- National network.
- Global network.

A complementary spatial network might be modeled as:

- House lot.
- Adjacent house lots.
- Neighborhood.
- City.
- Nation.
- World.

Returning to my example of Ballykilcline, Ireland, from Chapter 1, the social network would be something like:

- Individual tenant farmer.
- Nuclear family.
- Extended family.
- Farmers living nearby.
- Cohort of rent strikers.
- Tenants in County Roscommon.
- Merchants in Strokestown (the nearest market town).
- Landlord.

- Entire system of tenancy.
- British citizenry.

And the spatial network might be composed of:

- House lot and fields.
- Adjacent houses and fields.
- Townland residents' houses.
- Nearby non-townland residents.
- County residents.
- Province residents.
- Irish people.
- Members of the British Empire.

As noted, contextualized historical knowledge may be used to tie precise individuals and social groups to the various analytical frames. Despite the specific terms adopted, the point is that modern-world archaeology includes the concept of multidimensional network connections as a given in human history.

Network analysis requires acknowledging that relational ties link together the various levels of the network. An archaeologist with the ability to reconstruct a social network may wish to illustrate it with a sociogram and a graph diagram to show the relationships between the social and spatial networks. The combination of the two images, which may be difficult to express graphically, will represent the sociospatial network for a given place and time. Modern-world archaeologists must be able to model the actual connections between the nodes rather than simply assume their presence. Merely concluding that networks once existed is not enough; the actual linkages must be established by using anthropological, archaeological, historical, and geographical sources of information. That the precise connections may be difficult to determine with certainty merely reflects the complexities of historical network analysis.

Social connections might be rooted in personal esteem or respect, whereas the connections between social groups might rest on shared labor (as in the Maale example), real or imagined kinship or clan membership, or power relations (such as worker : owner, ruled : ruler). Geographically, the connections may be modeled as occurring within physical linkages, such as roads, pathways, canals, and bridges. An integral feature of the connection is that it must be understood as constituting a property of the linked nodes. In other words, the link itself cannot be ignored. A social connection described as mother : daughter is a feature of both individuals, just as a road connecting two rural villages is a feature of both villages. This understanding means that modern-world archaeologists must adapt their vision of space to include the connectors. Roads linking villages are features of the villages themselves and must be so considered. The Middle Passage that took millions of Africans across the Atlantic Ocean to the Americas connects the Old and New worlds.

Asymmetric connections, however, are quite possible. A daughter who feels slighted and abandoned by her mother may reject her mother's attempts to bond later in life. It may be possible that only a one-directional bond exists. Asymmetric ties are difficult to conceptualize in terms of physical space, but a good example is a swiftly running river that connects an upstream village with one downstream. In the absence of motorboats, the people living upstream may have connections with the people downstream, but the connection may not be reciprocal. The downstreamers may simply not have the technology to go upstream and the environment may preclude terrestrial travel. The upstream people may have more power than the downstream dwellers simply because they have greater access to resources. This historical reality may further complicate the asymmetric dimensions of the network connections, but the analyst must recognize them nonetheless.

One of the hallmarks of modern-world archaeology is that the application of network theory causes us to rethink our concepts of physical boundaries. Archaeologists are forced—when explicitly envisioning the relational ties between sites and people—to abandon their traditional understanding of what constitutes an archaeological site, area, or region. In keeping with the demands of network theory, archaeologists considering the connections between site dyads, triads, and networks must also acknowledge the physicality of the links themselves.

It is impossible in modern-world archaeology to imagine the African slave trade without the Atlantic Ocean, even though the ocean is often perceived metaphorically rather than materially. This large body of water tied the eighteenth century Caribbean islands to eighteenth century West Africa in historically relevant ways. Traditional historical archaeologists may consider West Africa and Jamaica to be two discrete places with two unique histories (perfectly acceptable on one scale), but modern-world archaeologists—following the lessons of network theory—refuse to ignore the Atlantic as the connector between the places. If we accept that the Atlantic is a characteristic of both network nodes, then we must acknowledge that a sociospatial region composed of Caribbean : Atlantic Ocean : West Africa must also have existed as a physical reality in eighteenth century global history.

Summary

Network theory provides a perspective that permits modern-world archaeologists to conceptualize sites in a new way. The linkages maintained by the people who lived in a past locale were connected socially and physically through personal linkages (kinship, friendship, work) and tangible works (roads, pathways, rivers). Modern-world archaeology posits that the archaeological vision must be expanded to include all relevant sociospatial links when attempting to interpret a past sociohistorical context. Failure to acknowledge the network connections and an unwillingness to appreciate the significance of these historical structures provide a flat—sometimes even ahistorical—interpretation that may provide more information about the analysts' views than about lived history itself. The application of network theory in modern-world archaeology makes it impossible to present analyses that perceive a household and its residents as unconnected to the many worlds that swirled around them. This perspective is one of the most important differences between modern-world archaeology and traditionally conceived historical archaeology.

WORLD–SYSTEMS ANALYSIS

World-systems analysis, like structural history and network theory, has spawned a large number of books and articles, with scholars from many academic fields adopting various points of view about its strengths and weaknesses. Unlike structural history and network theory, however, world-systems analysis has received considerably more attention from archaeologists eager to learn whether its ideas and concepts are useful to their interpretive efforts.

To understand the importance of world-systems analysis to modern-world archaeology, we must first acknowledge that two world(-)systems theories exist. The first, called world systems theory (without the hyphen), is associated with Andre Gunder Frank; the second, world-systems theory (with the hyphen), is associated with Immanuel Wallerstein. Archaeologists, including many who have used the ideas to investigate ancient pre-Columbian and Near Eastern societies, have adopted ideas from both strains of world(-)systems theory. Modern-world archaeology—because it concentrates on world history after 1500—is most associated with Wallerstein's model, even though Frank's basic position on broad-scale analysis is entirely consistent with modern-world archaeology.

Frank's World Systems Theory

The basis of Frank's world systems theory is that relations between centralized, powerful political entities and their considerably less powerful client polities have existed for many centuries. He first realized this while studying the unequal development that existed between First World metropolitan centers and their dependencies in the Global South (then termed the "Third World"). Being interested in long-term connections, Frank used archaeological and historical evidence from western and central Asia to bolster his argument. Documenting the presence of similar artifacts in

widely separated places, he argued that ancient peoples must have been interconnected across vast spaces as early as the Bronze Age. In network
terms the nodes (individual archaeological sites) had been connected via
historic links (trading routes) for centuries. Frank's view that networks had
operated for centuries prior to the creation of the "European miracle"
meant that Europe and capitalism were much less important to his overall
perspective.

Frank's last major work in long-term world systems research was *Re-
Orient: Global Economy in the Asian Age*. He argued in this book against
Braudel's perspective by positing that a massive global economy existed
long before Europeans had become involved in it. As a result he believed
that all scholars who promote the prominence of Europe in world history
are guilty of Eurocentrism. In his view Europe was a latecomer into the
globalized marketplace and its superpowers only filled in where China
and the Islamic world had once held dominance. In other words, Europe
simply grafted itself onto an already existing world economy rather than
having created something new.

The so-called "rise of the West" therefore cannot be understood without first acknowledging Africa, the Middle East, and especially China. Regarding China specifically, Frank demonstrated how the various royal
dynasties controlled the world market for decades by maintaining a complex collection of interregional networks. He proposed that the dominance
of Europe only occurred after about 1815, with the end of the Napoleonic
Wars. Europe was thus only a marginal player for most of world history
and was able to insert itself into world affairs only after China had begun
its nineteenth century decline.

Frank's comments about the significance of the distribution of porcelain throughout the world will resonate with historical archaeologists. His
research demonstrated that the Portuguese, Dutch, English, and other
major European powers were largely at the mercy of the powerful Chinese
dynasties that controlled not only the porcelain trade itself, but also access
to Chinese ports (see Chapters 6 and 7). Throughout its history the Ming
Dynasty held a monopoly on the production and trade of porcelain (not to
mention silk and other products equally desired by European consumers).
He argued that even the rise and fall of the Spanish Empire can be attributed to Asia because the Chinese demand for South American silver exerted severe pressures on the Spanish economy. Over time the increased
supply of silver depressed its price, resulting in the cost of production ex-
ceeding its value in exchange. Thus China (for Frank) was the engine of
global change far longer than Europe.

Besides Frank's specific views on the global significance of China in
the world economy and the persistence of a global economic system since
the Bronze Age, his methodological views are especially relevant to
modern-world archaeology. One of his central themes was that scholars
should adopt a worldwide view and cease concentrating so heavily on

Europe. For him a global understanding of the world constituted more than the sum of its parts; he believed that broad understandings could help us understand even the tiniest part of the whole. His model of society as a stool with three legs—composed of (a) ecology/economy/technology, (b) politics/military power, and (c) society/culture/ideology—had unacknowledged affinity with Braudel's model.

Wallerstein's World-System Analysis

Much of Frank's perspective in favor of Asia (really China) instead of Europe was directed largely against Wallerstein's world-systems theory. Wallerstein famously posits that the true world-economy developed only since the sixteenth century, largely as a result of European expansion. This "modern world-system" has at its base three specific features: (a) a single expanding economy (capitalism); (b) multiple states that expand through space; and (c) a specific capital : labor relation (owner : worker).

Critics often overlook the meaning of "world" in Wallerstein's framework and equate it with the globe. For him, however, a world-system represents a network that creates and maintains a world of its own within which its rules operate, rather than a unified system that exists simultaneously throughout the entire globe. His world is simply composed of those parts connected in a network.

World-systems analysis posits that only two varieties of world-systems have existed in world history: world-empires (such as the Roman Empire) and world-economies (such as European capitalism). World-empires are large bureaucratic sociopolitical structures that have a single political center and a single division of labor. They operate in many cultures, stretching their rules and regulations across them. A world-economy has a single division of labor but multiple political centers located in multiple cultures. The world-economy of most interest to Wallerstein, and also to modern-world archaeology, is the capitalist world-economy.

The capitalist world-economy is distinguished by a system of production organized around profitable exchange within a market economy. Using a general model devised by Marx, world-systems analysts begin by seeing the capitalist mode of production as being divided between individuals who own the means of production (tools, facilities, expertise) and workers who sell their labor and use the means of production to create things for the owners. For all its economic power to distribute a society's material resources, the world-economy is not political per se. Rather, the world-economy has an overarching economic structure but no consistent political framework. The integration of the capitalist world-economy is sustained by the economic interdependence—the network relations—constructed between the various political units involved. This interlinkage, however, need not be formalized with true political alliances. Instead the connection between political entities can be implied through simple practice. The rise of so-called "late capitalism" in recent years has demonstrated quite clearly that the most powerful multinational corporations can exist outside of and above the political realities of the world's nation-states.

Core : periphery relations (the dyadic, triadic, and multilevel linkages of network theory) provide an important central tenet of world-systems analysis. In the capitalist world-economy, the cores are central places from which production and capital emanate, whereas the peripheries are places that are dependent on the cores. Periphery dependency is of central importance because the linkage is inherently unequal (it constitutes an asymmetric network relation). In capitalist core : periphery relations, the cores are typically urban centers where the processes of production and exchange are monopolized and hence profitable. Owners of the means of production living in cores become wealthy through the sale of surplus values (profits over and above the cost of production, marketing, and sale). The workers in peripheries are not able to realize huge profits from their labors, so they are considerably poorer than the owners living in the cores; they are even poorer than the cores' agents living alongside them. The capitalist world-economy, by definition situated in post-Columbian history, operates through the inequalities built into the structure of the system itself. Post-Columbian (European) cores were state-level cultural polities, whereas the (non-European) peripheries were non-state-level polities. In this model weak states (called "semi-peripheries") are usually designated "colonies," because colonialism and imperialism are often part of the process.

Critics of world-systems analysis often overlook the multidimensional character of Wallerstein's model. Many of them incorrectly argue that the model is "totalizing" or that it ignores the highly localized sites that archaeologists study. But the contrary is true: Wallerstein's model provides the basis for modern-world archaeology in a fashion entirely consistent with Braudel's multiscalar model. Wallerstein believes that households represent the base-level unit of the world-system. The household is the place where individuals are socialized, where they learn both what is expected of them and what is possible for them given their position in the social hierarchy.

It is within this sociospatial setting—this specialized network having horizontal and vertical connections—that a person learns the social rules as well as the social boundaries within which he or she must live. Part of the socialization process involves learning the social hierarchies as well as internalizing the myths and ideologies of the world-economy. For instance, Americans are constantly taught that "all men are created equal," even though the reality is that some people are more equal than others. But because socialization is never total, some of the learning that takes place in a household may also include lessons about rebellion and resistance. Such contrary lessons are likely to be designated deviant or even illegal by those who control the social hierarchy and occupy its highest positions. Individuals in power can legislate against actions that would create freedom from oppression and in the process reaffirm and strengthen the structures they have created. Rebellious action can be made illegal by elites seeking to shape the life-long perspectives of those located beneath them in the social hierarchy.

Classes and other social groups are situated above the household in Wallerstein's model. These are collective creations that work to develop and maintain network relations between households ("trans-household institutions"). Above these institutions are states (political entities), corporate entities (economic and, today, increasingly extra-political entities), and the world-economy (the globalized structure of the capitalist project).

For Wallerstein classes and other groups existing within the capitalist world-economy are impacted by two widely divergent ideologies that compete for dominance: "universalism" and racism/sexism. Universalism is the understanding that the rules of society apply to all individuals equally and that they constitute the "official gospel of modernity." For example, universalism within the educational field posits that individuals obtain academic appointment based on their training, competence, and promise as scholars. The secret truth of today's practices, however, has much more to do with the cultural capital attached to one's advanced degree. A degree from an elite, private (and hence expensive) university holds much more cultural capital than a degree from a state university, regardless of the actual quality of the education received.

In a democratic nation, universalism may refer to "one person, one vote" regardless of the individual's sex, religion, or ethnicity. Universalism is intended as a positive feature of the capitalist world-economy but its ideological elements are more plainly evident in its antitheses—racism and sexism. Both racism and sexism are divisive ranking systems with enormous consequences for the operation of the capitalist world-economy, because each has the power to categorize individuals and groups as inferior. In my perspective sexism is a form of racialization because some people (women) are ranked as inferior due to a particular characteristic (their gender).

Summary

Two kinds of world(-)systems analysis have been proposed by scholars intent on understanding how the world's peoples have been interconnected through time. Frank's view about the long-term presence of such connections provides an important metaphor for modern-world archaeology. Many of his views, and especially his methods, deserve consideration. Some scholars have strongly criticized his picture of Chinese history as inconsistent and even incorrect in significant ways. Modern-world archaeology accepts Frank's understanding of large-scale connections and their tenacity through time, but it relies more strongly on Wallerstein's world-systems analysis because of its direct pertinence to post-Columbian history. The use of Wallerstein's models in modern-world archaeology derives from his interest in capitalism, one of the haunts of modern-world archaeology. Modern-world archaeology holds as a central tenet that post-Columbian history cannot be studied in any thorough manner without considering the actions and implications of the capitalist project.

DIALECTICAL THINKING

Structural history, network theory, and world-systems analysis can be said to incorporate relational thinking as a basic premise. For each of them to make sense, one must have an understanding of relationships because each one inherently models connections in generally consistent ways. In network theory, for instance, two nodes (a and b) take connector x as a primary attribute of their condition. The dyad $a : b$ cannot exist without x—thus $a : (x) : b$. By the same token, social time is impossible without individual time and a core cannot exist without peripheries. The entities are defined by their relations.

It is wholly inadequate, however, simply to note the relational characteristics of the various entities without having a firm understanding of the true nature of the relationships among them. Put another way, we must understand the theory of linkage to comprehend the constitution of the networks. In this sense our interest is much less on the nodes and much more on the relations that connect them (the links or edges). Dialectical thinking, as presented by Marx and best explained by political scientist Bertell Ollman, offers an excellent means for understanding linkage. I adopt Marx's dialectical method because modern-world archaeology is partly based on the investigation of capitalism, or what I term the "capitalist project" to suggest its extra-economic impacts. Few scholars have understood capitalism as profoundly or as completely as Marx. As a philosophical subject alone, dialectics is extremely complex, but it can be applied in a basic form to modern-world archaeology without having to delve too deeply into its considerable philosophical nuances.

Dialectical thinking has a long history going back to Plato. Scholars usually associate its more modern permutations with the works of German philosopher Georg Wilhelm Friedrich Hegel, and it was to him that Marx responded in his own understanding of dialectics. In the afterword to the second German edition of *Capital*, published in 1873, Marx drew a distinction between Hegel's dialectics and his own. He refers to Hegel's dialectics as "mystical" because of his reliance on idealism, and he noted that for Hegel "the Idea" takes precedence over "the real world." Being solidly grounded in materialism, Marx thus perceived his type of dialectics as the opposite of Hegel's. For him the idea "is nothing else than the material world reflected by the human mind and translated into forms of thought." Marx argued that Hegel's "mystical" form of dialectics upholds and glorifies the status quo, while his own "rational" dialectics has the power to reveal how the status quo was created and maintained. As a result Marx acknowledged that his brand of dialectics would be despised by "bourgeoisdom and its doctrinaire professors."

Marx drew an important theoretical distinction between his and Hegel's mode of dialectical thinking by observing that Hegel's mystical form was synchronic, whereas his focuses simultaneously on the state of things (the status quo) and the non-state of things (the status quo that could be). In other words, because Marx perceived "every historically developed social form as in fluid movement"—that is, that all historical moments are in a constant state of change (today a stalwart principle of anthropological reasoning)—he understood that the state of things would soon become its negation, that the "momentary existence" of a social form would soon evolve into another form. Thus the roots of the "status quo that could be" exist within "the status quo that is." And because he was dedicated to the transformation of society from capitalism to socialism, Marx understood that his concept of dialectical thinking was "critical and revolutionary" (1967 [1867], Vol. I, pp. 12–20).

Marx's Dialectics

Marx's understanding is appealing to archaeological analysis because he conceived the static and the fluid as part of the same historical moment. This perspective helps us understand the complex nature of human society as it is actually lived: as a complex series of trans-temporal networks within which the interactions of our time are inexorably linked to both the past (the time that was) and the future (the time that will be) all at once. When studied in the past, dialectical relations have the appearance of processes (because they can be observed over different lengths of time). The starting point of a Marxian dialectical study is the present, which for Marx was nineteenth century capitalism and for us is the early twenty-first century. Analysis then proceeds backward in time from there.

Marx believed that to examine the capitalist present one first must understand how capitalism actually operates, which involves grasping the relations between the two gross classes involved in production (workers and owners). Using network theory, we can easily model workers and owners as nodes in a network tied together with the relevant productive relations. For example, workers on an automobile assembly line (a) would be linked to the factory's owners (b) through the rules, standards, and production speeds (x) established by the owners and enforced by intermediary managers—thus $a : (x) : b$. Moreover, all these nodes would be connected materially through the machinery (y_1) and the cars (y_2) themselves—thus $a : (xy_1 + xy_2) : b$.

Once the task of understanding how capitalist relations are established and maintained is accomplished, the next task is to understand their pre-

conditions. Marx took this to mean that he had to investigate the productive relations embedded within European feudalism, the mode of production that immediately preceded mercantilism. His comments in this regard
are particularly important to appreciating his method because he noted that
we must adopt a multiscalar approach that views historical time bidirec-
tionally; the past is forever linked to our present. In other words, nineteenth
century productive relations (modeled as horizontal network connections)
are connected to feudalism (modeled as vertical network connections).
Marx's vertical connections also extend into the unknowable future, when
he believed people would band together to create true socialism.

Using the development of humanity as an example, Marx explained
that the existence of humanity is the result of earlier processes through
which organic life had to pass. Humankind could only appear once a certain point had been reached in this organic process. Once humans existed
they became both the permanent product and the result of human history.
Humankind thus constitutes its own precondition. Capitalism developed
in the same manner, with capital having to begin as a "parting product"
from the dissolution of feudalism (the preceding historical epoch). Like-
wise, the precondition of future socialism already exists—lying dormant—
within today's capitalism, and so one must study feudalism to understand
capitalism. (For this reason I have noted that modern-world archaeology
can extend further back into history than the year 1500, even though the
vast bulk of the research is centered on post-1500 history.) It would do little good, therefore, to understand capitalism as an economic system that
"simply is." One key to understanding it is to study its precursor or, in
other words, what it is not.

From the perspective of dialectical thinking, the study of feudalism
is never just about medieval history. It cannot be removed from its transformation into capitalism. Capitalism is feudalism and feudalism is capitalism. The dialectical study of European feudalism is always about
capitalism; the examination of capitalism is always about feudalism. In
modern-world archaeology the corollary is that a single archaeological
property cannot be studied in a sociohistorical void, neatly removed from
its horizontal and vertical network connections. The examination of a
seventeenth century Dutch fort on the coast of Brazil cannot be removed
from the mercantile history that came before it (and created its conditions)
and the capitalist history that came after it (for which it created conditions).

Marx's entire intellectual life was spent closely examining capitalism,
but his dialectical method can be applied to any sociohistorical situation because it revolves around understanding the totality while at the same time
being robust enough to admit the particular and the unique. Marx was
deeply engaged in understanding the universalizing power of the capitalist project in order to overthrow it. His dialectics allowed him to comprehend that the roots of its destruction already existed within it. Capitalism's

ability as a world-economy to create and maintain a complex web of structurally identical relations throughout the world, however, does not mean that particularlized sociohistorical realities must be ignored. Quite the contrary, the application of dialectical thinking means that the universalized and the particular (the global and the local) are integral parts of one another. In Marx's dialectical framework, the particular is the universal and the universal is the particular; neither exists alone. This is the perspective accepted in modern-world archaeology.

Summary

Dialectics constitutes a complex body of philosophical thought and I make no claim to know its entire history or to understand its many subtle nuances. What I wish to take from this body of thinking, however, is that the particular and the universal are intimately linked and that each contains elements of the other within it. It would make little sense to perceive the relationships forged by an eighteenth century French fur trader with Canadian First Nations in the absence of understanding the wider relationships that made these connections significant in the first place. And it makes little sense to address the conditions and concerns of First Nations today by ignoring their history. From the standpoint of modern-world archaeology, it is virtually impossible to conceptualize an individual archaeological site in the absence of the wider world; the wider world is the archaeological site, and the archaeological site is the wider world. The residents of a single household were citizens of the world, even if they did not appreciate what this meant.

As a final point, Terry Eagleton's observation in *Why Marx Was Right* is well worth considering.

Modernity is not to be mindlessly celebrated, but neither is it to be disdainfully dismissed. Its positive and negative qualities are for the most part aspects of the same process. This is why only a dialectical approach, one which grasps how contradiction is of its essence, can do it justice. (2011, p. 41)

An important goal of modern-world archaeology is to use dialectical thinking to acknowledge, understand, and challenge the haunts—both in the past and in the present.

CONCLUSION

In this chapter I have outlined the four foundational pillars of modern-world archaeology. Each one taken individually is important in its own right, and the body of literature that has grown up around each aptly demonstrates the interpretive power contained within them individually. None of them were devised or developed with archaeological research in mind, even though each one contains elements that have significant archaeological relevance.

Structural history offers a framework for analysis that is multiscalar and profoundly historical in orientation. Braudel's studies demonstrate the value of intensive historical research while also presenting an overarching worldview tying the local to the global and the global to the local. Network theory offers a conceptual framework for understanding how networks operate and challenges investigators to understand that the characteristics of the nodes also include the characteristics of the links. A network without links is impossible. World-systems analysis further expands Braudel's analyses and stresses the ways in which broad historical linkages have blanketed the world at various times in the past. Wallerstein's analyses specifically explore and explain the world-system of the capitalist world-economy, and Marx's dialectics helps us conceptualize how relationships actually work.

Modern-world archaeology, above all, is based on the concept of multiscalar relations. No archaeological site, no matter how remote or short term, can be perceived as acting outside the world of social and environmental networks (horizontal and vertical). Rather, the concepts contained within structural history, network theory, world-systems analysis, and dialectical thinking can be united in various ways—with each application serving together to help us interpret discrete sociohistorical settings. The combination of these four bodies of thought helps us understand the world in which we live and accept the impacts of its prior worlds.

SUGGESTED READINGS

Structural History

Bintliff, John (editor) 1991. *The Annales School and Archaeology.* New York University Press, New York.
　　A number of studies in which archaeologists have employed Braudel's concepts.

Braudel, Fernand. 1972. *The Mediterranean and the Mediterranean World in the Age of Philip II.* Translated by Siân Reynolds. Harper Colophon, New York.

Braudel, Fernand. 1973. *Capitalism and Material Life, 1400–1800.* Translated by Miriam Kochan. Harper & Row, New York.

Braudel, Fernand. 1985. *Civilization and Capitalism, 15th-18th century.* 3 vols. Translated by Siân Reynolds. Harper & Row, New York.

Three books that present Braudel's most important thoughts on structural history. Must reading.

Radcliffe-Brown, A. R. 1940. On Social Structure. *Journal of the Royal Anthropological Society of Great Britain and Ireland* 70:1–12.

A key statement about how societies construct social organizations by one of the major figures in the history of anthropology. Also, an early mention of the importance of network concepts in understanding social structures.

Network Theory

Knappett. Carl. 2012. *An Archaeology of Interaction: Network Perspectives on Material Culture and Society*. Oxford University Press, Oxford, UK.

An important overview of the role of network theory in archaeology using Old World examples.

Padgett, John F., and Christopher K. Ansell. 1993. Robust Action and the Rise of the Medici, 1400–1434. *American Journal of Sociology* 98:1259–1319.

A historical network analysis using the Medicis of Florence as a case study.

Scott, John G. 1991. *Social Network Analysis: A Handbook*. Sage, London.

A short, easy-to-understand presentation of the basics of social network analysis.

Wasserman, Stanley, and Katherine Faust. 1994. *Social Network Analysis: Methods and Applications*. Cambridge University Press, Cambridge, UK.

A definitive study of social network theory from simple to complex.

World-Systems Analysis

Frank, Andre Gunder. 1993. Bronze Age World System Cycles. *Current Anthropology* 34:383–429.

Frank, Andre Gunder. 1998. *ReOrient: Global Economy in the Asian Age*. University of California Press, Berkeley.

Two works presenting Frank's view of the world systems that have operated since the Bronze Age.

Wallerstein, Immanuel. 1974. *The Modern World-System I: Capitalist Agriculture and the Origins of the European World-Economy in the Sixteenth Century*. Academic Press, New York.

Wallerstein, Immanuel. 1980. *The Modern World-System II: Mercantilism and Consolidation of the European World-Economy, 1600–1750*. Academic Press, New York.

Two in-depth analyses of the modern world-system.

Wallerstein, I. 2004. *World-Systems Analysis: An Introduction.* Duke University Press, Durham, NC.
    A short, very readable introduction to world-systems analysis.

Dialectical Thinking

Eagleton, Terry. 2011. *Why Marx Was Right.* Yale University Press, New Haven, CT.
    A good, short study of the significance of Marx's analyses to today's world situation.

Ollman, Bertell. 2003 [1993]. *Dance of the Dialectic: Steps in Marx's Method.* University of Illinois Press, Urbana, IL.
    An excellent explanation of Marx's often difficult-to-understand dialectical method.

STUDY QUESTIONS

1. Provide a historical example where it would be insightful to use Braudel's different scales. What might we learn from each one that is different from the others?

2. Draw a sociogram of your circle of friends showing both strong and weak links.

3. Explain the basic differences between world systems theory and world-systems theory.

4. In terms of dialectical thinking, what does it mean to say that "masters need slaves in order to be masters"?

CHAPTER 4

STRUCTURES

I observed in Chapter 2 that the haunts float around in the background of archaeology, simultaneously affecting both its practical application (its methods) and the ways in which archaeologists assess and interpret history (its theories). The haunts' ghostly substance, however, should not lead us to suppose that their agents work in the absence of overarching frameworks or that they are completely free to weave the fabric of life unfettered by societal constraints. Such an understanding of the philosophical concept of agency may make us believe that individualism is a human universal rather than a feature of political rhetoric and nationalist ideology. Carried to its extreme, the concept of agency applied in this manner tacitly references the neoliberal view that perceives individuals as having perfect freedom to act as they wish. The perception that human agency is unbounded by the social strictures in which actual individuals operate is part of the neoliberal mantra that people have the opportunity to "raise themselves up by their own bootstraps." Failure to do so is thus purely the individual's fault. To think this way denies the ideological power of elites and their agents to control, though it does not eliminate rebellion and revolt from below.

EPOCHAL STRUCTURES

The agents of colonialism, Eurocentrism, capitalism, and racialization designed conceptual parameters to guide their actions—even if it may appear in hindsight that they "made it up as they went along." Every haunt, as well as the subprocesses constructed within them, has a consciously constructed framework that limits and guides daily social interaction and reproduces social relationships through time. The agents of the haunts have built frameworks upon which they have hung the principles, practices, and meanings imagined and conceived by society's ruling elites. These structures have dialectical characteristics that allow them to change over time while retaining their basic structure.

Following Donham (see Chapter 3), I refer to these frameworks as epochal structures. His idea evokes Bourdieu's concept of *habitus*, in which individuals living in a social structure have agency, but only as it is limited by the parameters of their social situation (see Chapter 6). And as Bourdieu showed, the presence of epochal structures does not mean that people cannot struggle against the structures, manipulate them for their own purposes, or even modify them in some cases (see Chapter 7). But tenacity and a certain degree of rigidity is a key feature of an epochal structure and modern-world archaeology seeks to investigate these structures.

Epochal structures are relational. They appear in the social world as relations between individuals and groups, in the physical (including ecological) world as relations between things, and in the sociospatial world as relations between people and things. In truth, all relations are sociospatial and describe the sociospatial dialectic, because all humans (and even animals and plants) cannot interact outside physical space except conceptually. Each physical setting interacts with living organisms as much as living things interact with it. The guiding idea underlying sociospatial dialectics is that people produce space through their relationships as an inherent element of those relationships. Any effort to separate them is thus purely artificial and mostly done for analytical purposes.

EPOCHAL STRUCTURES AND HUMAN AGENCY

My understanding of epochal structures derives from the work of anthropologist Donald Donham, who studied the Maale of southern Ethiopia. The Maale, who number about 15,000 people, are slash-and-burn horticulturalists who inhabit the edge of today's global capitalist system. Donham's particular interest is to understand their mode of production and how it shapes cultural power and ideology. A major component of his research revolves around the Maale's epochal structures.

Donham models epochal structures as top-down frameworks created by power elites who promote them as "simply the way things are." They are ideological, historical, and rooted in power relations. Individuals living within the confines of the structures are not completely powerless because they have some latitude of action. Their actions, however, take place within the limits established by the powerful. As a result the dominant group has the power and authority to reward and punish as it strives to convince the dominated that the dominant's interests are the same as everyone's. It would be easy to suppose that individuals living within the structure have no personal will, but it remains true that power distinctions rooted in the materiality of everyday life define the epochal structures. Thus the acquisition and application of power establishes both the structure itself and the parameters of action within the structure.

The long-term stability and solidity of an epochal structure derive from the elite's use of the coercive and ideological forces at its command. In this sense we may view the structure's operation through time as representing a vertical network whose power and authority is established as tradition and is viewed ideologically as timeless. As evidenced by the European concept of the divine right of kings, the final ideological authority may come from an imagined deity. Stripped of its ideology, though, the claims of the dominant group in a great many cases often fraudulently represent the general public's interest.

As used by Donham, the concept of agency has two senses, each of which is situated inside the broader concept of the epochal structure. The concept of "epochal agency" appears in the patterns of individual action that are motivated by culturally relevant meanings and practices. These actions and their meanings operate to maintain the framework of the epochal structure. If we think in terms of a physical scaffold, individuals practicing epochal agency would be the construction personnel who ensure that the framework is in good working order and that it is stable enough to stand through time. They might replace worn-out beams and braces and make certain that the boards on the platforms are in good repair. "Historical agency" is different because it involves struggles against the epochal structure. These struggles occur in discrete places and at discernable periods of time, but their ultimate goal is to question the inequalities built into the structure itself. Their efforts may or may not be successful in causing lasting change to occur, but when change does occur its effects probably will not alter the overall design of the structure.

To return to our hypothetical scaffold, individuals practicing historical agency might arrive in the dead of night, steal onto the construction site, and attempt to dismantle the framework. They might be successful in removing some of the levels of the scaffold; they may even topple the entire structure. The next morning, however, the agents practicing epochal agency will return and reconstruct the scaffold, perhaps making it even stronger and more difficult to dismantle. This act of reconstruction does not mean that the agents of historical agency will not reappear and try again, but it does demonstrate the tenacity of the epochal structure. The owners of the scaffolding—a construction or engineering company or perhaps even a municipality—simply have greater resources on their side, often including the authority of the law as well. The aggregate power supports the building and maintenance of the scaffolding and ensures that it stands as long as needed.

The Maale's Structures

During his fieldwork Donham learned that the Maale's method of horticultural production had remained fairly stable from the late nineteenth to
the mid-twentieth centuries. Their means of production were technologi-
cally so basic that only a few individuals owned metal tools. Work tasks
were gender-specific (men were assigned some tasks and women others)
as well as gendered (the tasks were viewed as "male" or "female" tasks)
and gendering (an individual of either sex performing a "male" task was
considered male). Female labor included collecting firewood and water,
caring for children, and cooking meals, whereas the males' tasks involved
hunting, caring for livestock, and keeping bees. Males and females had to
reaffirm their individual gender roles by performing tasks deemed proper
for each gender. Sexual designation could be entirely based on work, such
that any female who hunted could be considered male and a man who
cooked could be considered female.

Maale society included a complex mixture of social inequalities based
on tribute, lineage, domestic unit, and caste. These vectors of inequality
defined the epochal structure and each of their substructures was interwoven and inseparable. In this sense the concept of the epochal structure
(though explained in the Maale's noncapitalist setting) is completely compatible with the four haunts, because each haunt can be discussed as if it
were an individual substructure within the larger post-Columbian superstructure. In the post-Columbian modern world, the substructures interact and conjoin in innumerable complex ways that are impossible to
separate except artificially.

One of the key elements of epochal structures is that they must be re-
producible. They must be relatively stable over time and allow for the creation and continuance of sustainable structures of social relations. The
ideology of fetishization provides one mechanism for promoting the perceived stability of the structure. Donham discovered, for example, that the
Maale fetishized fertility rather than commodities (as in capitalism). Their
"fertility fetishism" was based on horticulture and hunting. Commoners
were not permitted to plant their fields before the king had planted his.
Chiefs and subchiefs took tribute to the king at the end of the dry season
and the king began to pray to his ancestors for rain. When the rains came,
the chiefs ordered the subchiefs to send commoners to the king's fields to
plant his crops. The chiefs could plant only after the king's fields were fully
sown, and the subchiefs could plant only after the chiefs' fields were completed. The senior elder of a commoner descent group could plant after the
subchiefs, with the junior elders following them. The heads of the minor
lineages then sowed their fields and the commoners planted last.

The Maale reproduced this complex system of horticultural ordering
through the understanding that no individual is truly an isolated person set
off from other individuals. Instead each person conceptualized his or her

"place" within a hierarchical, multiscalar network that extended upward from individual to lineage to chiefdom to kingdom. Individuals maintained specific social relations at each level: with elders, ancestors, the lineage founder, subchiefs, chiefs, and king.

The Maale example amply demonstrates that epochal structures have unique characteristics depending upon historical, cultural, and social contexts. A universal, timeless model of *the* epochal structure—especially one applicable to both pre- and post-Columbian, noncapitalist and capitalist sociohistorical situations—can never be created. That said, however, the union of the four haunts around 1500 has created an epochal structure that has endured with significant modifications for about five hundred years. Capitalism has expanded throughout the globe and spread its ideology of the availability of individual wealth. Eurocentric ideals of beauty pervade the media. Racialization is still with us and innumerable people across the world still wrestle with the residues of colonialism, imperialism, and empire. Critics may conclude that modern-world archaeology is totalizing, but for me this critique ignores verifiable history.

A BRIEF EXAMPLE FROM THE SOUTHERN UNITED STATES

A detailed exploration of any of the four haunts can illustrate the importance of understanding the concept of the epochal structure, but here I focus specifically on racialization in the antebellum American South. The reproduction of this epochal structure, at least as it pertains to the history of the United States, is relatively easy to conceptualize because of the continuing significance of race in American society. Without question racial designation remains a tenacious and contentious issue for contemporary Americans, just as it has been for generations. The example of antebellum racialization is also useful because the image of the American South figures so prominently, rightly or wrongly, in the historical ideology and national psyche of the United States.

Antebellum Plantation Structures

In the years preceding the American Civil War, the social structure in the southern slave-holding states—though not entirely static—was composed of two diametric (and somewhat idealized) categories of people based upon perceived physical appearance and cultural characteristics. Those at the top of the structure were self-designated as white and (at the pinnacle) Anglo-Saxon, whereas those at the bottom of the structure were designated nonwhite and decidedly non-Anglo-Saxon. (Various others, such as German immigrants, were in the middle.) White individuals engaged in the region's agricultural production were arranged into the following social categories:

Figure 7. A large slaveowner's house.

- Large planters (land-rich enslavers).
- Small planters and commercial farmers (landed enslavers and non-enslavers).
- Yeoman farmers (landed or renting and generally non-enslavers).
- Landless laborers (non-landed, non-enslavers).

The ranks were hierarchical, such that "southern gentlemen" were situated at the apex of the structure. Apologists for the region's dominant ideology generally described these men in the glowing terms we now think of as stereotypic: virtuous, courteous, and gentlemanly. These individuals upheld the structure that existed below them, partly by designating all people of color—even those who were legally free—as inferior. The white/nonwhite separation was usually more important to the elites than the free/enslaved division, in that they could discriminate against free African Americans as easily as they could against the enslaved.

Elite plantation owners generally considered the bondspeople on their estates to be divided into a hierarchy based upon the perceived value of the labor each performed. Thus the owners valued house servants—men and women in direct contact with the planters' families—more highly than their field hands, many of whom they may not even have known (at least on the largest estates). The social distinction was usually also obvious in housing, such that elites lived in big houses (Figure 7) and people in bondage lived in much smaller and less permanent buildings (Figure 8). The structural relationship between the owner and the enslaved was simply master : slave, even though personal bonds were often created between individuals. Even within the repressive institution of the plantation, however, owners and their agents learned that they had to practice social control carefully. In giving advice about the "proper" handling of the enslaved on large estates, planters were cautioned to use coercion discretely. The wisest owners combined firmness with a patronizing understanding that as white men of wealth they were innately superior to their dark-skinned "charges."

The slave-based epochal structure of the antebellum plantation was a design that if perfectly followed should lead to a tranquil and productive estate. The overriding goal of the structure was to produce economic profit for the owner with the least possible cost, and peaceful social relations (backed up with fear of punishment and perhaps death) would help ensure this outcome. All the owner's labors—both personal and combined with those of other southern plantation owners—can be considered examples of epochal agency.

Figure 8. Small, impermanent duplex houses of the enslaved.

Historians have long debated whether the antebellum plantation constituted a capitalist institution. This debate may never be resolved to everyone's satisfaction, but one thing is clear: owners had the accumulation of
wealth as their central concern and were dedicated to ensuring that their
designed epochal structure was in place as long as possible. In fact, it took
a devastating civil war to dismantle the structure of slavery—if not the
structure of racialization itself.

Dual Structures

In the context of the antebellum southern epochal structure, it is interesting to ponder the presence of another social structure that operated sur-
reptitiously within it. Research has shown that the enslaved maintained
their own structure, probably unknown to the plantation owners and overseers. The enslaved designed this structure in such a way that the individuals at the top possessed skills and characteristics they admired, such as
conjuring and midwifery. At the bottom were individuals whom the community generally despised, such as voluntary concubines and informants.
All other individuals were ranked into social positions based upon their
service to the community in a system that ran directly counter to the elite's
epochal structure. In the enslaved community, rebels—individuals who
were routinely vilified, tortured, and often killed by the owners—were
ranked near the top, even though their actions could cause severe retribu-
tion by the planters. The enslaved who struggled against the slave regime
practiced historical agency because they worked within the structure to
shake its foundations and dismantle as much of it as possible.

The presence of dual structures existing within the large antebellum
plantations of the American South is an interesting and important phenomenon, but can the structure created within a slave community be considered an epochal structure? Two reasons suggest why this designation
would be incorrect. First, the slave-designed system was not created and
enforced with a coercive power that could have wide societal impact. True,
individuals in the community could retaliate against informers or those
who were too friendly with the owners or overseers, and the enslaved did
frequently rebel (both overtly and covertly). Overall, however, their uprisings proved unsuccessful when viewed from a long-term perspective. Slave
revolts, even those that caused the dominant epochal structure to wobble—
such as the many uprisings in New York City between 1712 and 1741—did
not cause it to crack and fall. If anything, disturbances on the part of the enslaved provided excuses for the powerful to expand their authority and increase the terror they exercised over those whom they dominated.

Second, any social structure that operated within a slave community
was not an epochal structure because it did not persist through time. Most
disintegrated with the death of slavery, even though the elite's epochal

structure continued to operate. The racially based structure did not collapse at the end of the Civil War but simply continued in a transformed manner. Plantation owners always had a structural place for those who labored for them. After 1865 they sought to replace the African Americans whom they had once owned with "docile" Asian "coolies" and "hardy" Europeans, variously from Sweden, Norway, Germany, Ireland, Spain, France, and Italy. Planters tended to believe that these immigrant groups could be manipulated and controlled through the process of debt peonage. And because they were wage laborers rather than true slaves, planters were not required to expend their profits for their maintenance. Having failed in their efforts to attract sufficient numbers of laborers willing to work long hours in often-trying circumstances, planters were forced to accept former bondsmen and bondswomen as tenant farmers, because these men and women had the knowledge and experience needed to raise southern crops.

The elites used their power, authority, and influence to maintain and enforce their racialized structure throughout the post-slavery transition, with those deemed white considered to have much greater social standing than those deemed nonwhite. The flood of immigrants beginning in the mid-nineteenth century did not significantly alter the nation's racialized epochal structure, as the power elites simply installed the new immigrants into inferior positions based on perceived non-Anglo-Saxon characteristics, practices, and cultural traditions. The inferior social positions imposed on non-English immigrants translated into demeaning, dangerous, and low-paying jobs. The race-based structure inherent in the assignment of white and nonwhite (or Anglo-Saxon/non-Anglo-Saxon) was inseparable from the necessities of capitalist work discipline in the United States.

EPOCHAL STRUCTURES AND THE HAUNTS

Students of twentieth and twenty-first century U.S. history have established that the race-based structural inequalities created earlier have continued to the present day. The tenacity of a race-based epochal substructure throughout American history—albeit with changing narratives and different contexts discoverable with analysis—amply demonstrates the fairly rigid frameworks that can be created and maintained through history, even though the names of the principal actors many change. The interlinkage of the four haunts (as a unified epochal structure) helps reinforce each substructure. The bondage of humans in colonial America and the United States was initially substantiated with the entwined understanding of the relationship between colonialism and Eurocentrism, just as the linkage between capitalism and racialization reinforced dominant ideas about the superiority of Europeans over non-Europeans—expressed in the United States as Anglo-Saxons over non-Anglo-Saxons.

It must be made abundantly clear, however, that epochal structures are created and enforced with elite power. This does not mean that individuals and groups are entirely powerless against the structures (see Chapter 7). Peoples practicing resistance can effect some changes in the structures, but the real question is just how much change they can truly inspire.

Racism

Without question the world inhabited by African Americans until 1964 was appreciably worse than it is as of this writing. Racism today is arguably more muted than it was then and more African Americans have positions of authority and respect in business, sports, politics, education, and other areas of American life. It is no longer unusual to see men and women of color fairly represented on television and in movies, and some of the most admired celebrities in the world are people of color. In 1950 this world seemed practically unimaginable.

Significant modifications to the racial substructure have occurred but the picture is not altogether rosy. Just to cite two brief examples:

• The U.S. Bureau of Justice Statistics reports that the rate of incarceration of black males is 6.5 times higher than that of white males, and that the rate of execution of black inmates is 4.5 times higher than that of whites.
• The Southern Poverty Law Center monitors the activities of several hundred hate groups in the United States that are avowedly (and proudly) racist, anti-Semitic, anti-Islamic, anti-immigrant, and anti-LGBT. Though most are fringe groups with little credibility, their continued presence (including in the media) suggests the structural reality of race-based separation.

Racist thinking continues to persist. Some studies, in fact, suggest it may even be on the rise. Why?

Two explanations may account for the persistence of racism. Either racism is part of "human nature" or it is structural. Without question all peoples throughout history have perceived foreigners to be different. Languages are unfamiliar, customs seem strange, and religions appear irrational. The central issue, however, is whether these differences have been ingrained within a society's dominant ideology. The persistence of Eurocentric beliefs and practices has been a significant part of the dominant ideology since at least 1500. People on the streets of seventeenth century Lisbon may have recognized the Africans among them as different on a personal level, but the primitive ethnographies written by Portuguese missionaries and explorers helped solidify the understanding that African customs and traditions were less desirable than European mercantilism and Roman Catholicism.

The many localized contacts, interactions, and exchanges (or avoidances), though they may have altered an individual's understanding of and appreciation for other cultures, did not have the power to alter the epochal structure. As a result the epochal structure of the European mindset remained intact. Curiously, in the twenty-first century many influential people still promote Eurocentric notions without the least sense of introspection, often cleverly adopting pseudoscience and religion to prop up their ideas.

CONCLUSION

My brief example of the antebellum slave-holding plantation requires much more contextualization to be entirely successful. Plantation housing is one place where the physicality of the antebellum epochal structure was and still is obvious. The stability of the epochal structure is observable today, just as it was in the past in the structures inhabited by plantation men, women, and children. The physical structures thus provide a useful metaphor for the invisible—though powerful—epochal structure itself.

The plantation homes of the wealthiest planters were places like those you may have seen in *Gone With the Wind*: huge, pillared homes reached by riding or walking through an avenue of magnificent trees. These homes, with their grand stairways and parquet-floored ballrooms, were often painted white to set them apart from the green environment. The houses of the residents at the bottom of the structure (the enslaved) were not as obvious. These small, impermanent, and insufficient homes may have sometimes been whitewashed inside, but their rough-hewn exteriors indicated that they were intended to be unnoticeable from afar. The houses inhabited by overseers, managers, and other non-enslaved workers were generally not as inadequate as those of the enslaved, but they were nowhere near as opulent as the mansions of the true elite. The homes of this middle group reflected the reality that they too were workers, like the enslaved; they were simply not in bondage.

The image I have drawn is again somewhat stereotypic: most planters lived relatively modestly, since only a tiny minority was truly wealthy. But it is interesting from the standpoint of the epochal structure to consider which houses still remain on the landscape. A few of the homes of the enslaved still exist here and there and the inquisitive archaeologist can sometimes locate one or two of them. On the other hand, tourists can easily visit the homes of the region's wealthiest planters. Their presence exhibits the permanence of the epochal structure, and the fact that many of them are open to the public—where the grand surroundings of the richest can be directly experienced today—attests to the staying power of the epochal structure.

My presentation is only intended to show that structures exist in the world and that peoples' lives function within them. The epochal structures can only be identified and understood using a conjunction of theory and empirical knowledge. We cannot see or touch these structures because they are no more tangible than racist belief. Like racism, we can only experience them through their expressions in the real world. Young families denied the purchase of a house because of the color of their skin or their religious beliefs feel the presence of racialization and Eurocentrism, even though they cannot touch them. The race-based social hierarchy is as real to them as it is to the white real estate agent who is guiding them to those parts of the city deemed "right" for them.

Each of the haunts has at least one epochal substructure. Other substructures may appear at deeper levels. For colonialism the coarsest structure consists of colonialist and colonized, and for Eurocentrism the structure sets Europeans apart from all other peoples. Capitalism divides owners from workers, just as racialization sets apart the "superior" from the "inferior." Viewed at closer frames, each of these structures will be found to have numerous permutations based on time and space. Even so, the basic structure of the dominant epochal structure remains stubbornly intact.

The post-1500 era is the time when the epochal substructures of the haunts were forced together to create a powerful superstructure defining the modern world. The haunts mesh to support and reinforce one another in a wholly innovative way. The epochal structure of capitalism merges with the structures of the other three haunts and is inseparable from them. Whether one of the structures seems to assume primacy at any particular historical moment is a function of the scale of analysis. We may wish to examine the racial structure imposed on one or several sugar-producing antebellum plantations, but this does not mean that the capitalist project has disappeared. Its effects are still there though they may not be the subject of analysis; they are simply not recognized by the analytical frame. European-style colonialism in the absence of Eurocentrism may be possible to imagine, and perhaps can even be investigated in this manner, but this level of analysis does not mean that the basic structure of Eurocentric practice is not present.

This analytical set is the basis for modern-world archaeology. The overall goal is to illuminate the material conditions of the modern world through the lens of the four haunts, without forgetting or ignoring the significance of particular sociohistorical contexts. Modern-world archaeologists use the intense perspective of microscale historical archaeology to build images of the recent past that hopefully have meaning to our present world. The goal, however, is to continue beyond the micro scale to provide analyses and interpretations that can help us know our broader global history. This, then, leads directly to an exploration of the role of microhistorical analysis in modern-world archaeology.

SUGGESTED READINGS

Bonilla-Silva, Eduardo. 1997. Rethinking Racism: Toward a Structural Interpretation. *American Sociological Review* 62:465–480.
An analysis of the structural nature of racism and racialization in the United States.

Donham, Donald L. 1999. *History, Power, Ideology: Central Issues in Marxism and Anthropology.* University of California Press, Berkeley.
The ethnographer's study of the Maale. Employs social network theory.

Lefebvre, Henri. 1991. *The Production of Space.* Edited and translated by Donald Nicholson-Smith. Blackwell, Oxford, UK.
A study of the ways in which social relations create physical space. A key to understanding sociospatial dialectics.

STUDY QUESTIONS

1. Consider the concept of the epochal structure and decide whether or not a university may constitute an example.

2. Think of an example of historical agency as it might relate to an antebellum plantation in the American South.

3. Give two reasons why you think epochal structures last through time and state why you think they are difficult to undo.

4. Explain how epochal structures intersect with racialization as it pertains to the poor in the United States.

CHAPTER 5

MICROHISTORY

One of the major misconceptions about modern-world archaeology is that it is dedicated solely to the study of the global at the expense of the local. One view is that in using world-systems analysis modern-world archaeologists overlook the particularity of the single site, the sole household, and the unique trash pit. I have attempted to dispel this misunderstanding in the preceding chapters. My comments about the need for multiscalar analysis and the requirement of looking at the small and unique in order to link it to the global should have dispelled this mischaracterization.

Nonetheless, the view that modern-world archaeology cannot focus on single sites is a persistent misinterpretation. Modern-world archaeology in no way denies the significance of site-specific (or micro) studies in historical archaeology. Site-specific studies constitute the basic information of all archaeological research, regardless of the eventual scope of analysis. The unavoidable fact is that the excavation of discrete places provides the archaeologist's core information. The key question is what happens to the site information once it has been excavated, analyzed, and stored away. Can it accomplish more than reveal the past at a single site?

I answer this question throughout this book. But the issue of site-specific studies raises concerns that must be addressed. Many historical archaeologists writing single-site studies stress the historical nature of the place by providing narratives that outline and recount the chronology of events that occurred there. They typically derive this background material from a union of primary and secondary historical sources, often acting as traditional historians. Like historians, historical archaeologists regularly thumb through deeds and other land records, decipher faded letters and diaries, correlate old maps with present-day landforms, and compile oral histories from the living. Much of this historical research, when focused on one place, could easily fall under the rubric of microhistory.

In this chapter I explore the relationships between microhistory and modern-world archaeology, as a multiscalar historical archaeology of the past five centuries. In many ways microhistorical studies approximate archaeologists' site-specific studies, but without the excavations that accompany them. An examination of microhistory has the advantage of demonstrating how modern-world archaeology, even though it has overt extra-site interests, can use its methods and perspectives to provide more thoroughly contextualized analyses.

One of the intriguing features of microhistory is that many of its practitioners have used an analogy with archaeology to describe their methods. Microhistorians often speak of excavating archives, sifting through documents like excavators, and unearthing the "relics" of everyday lived history. These archaeological analogies may simply reflect the loose usage of the terms, but in *The Cheese and the Worms: The Cosmos of a Sixteenth-Century Miller* Carlo Ginzburg—a leading figure in microhistory—made the connection between microhistory and archaeology explicit. "Since historians are unable to converse with the peasants of the sixteenth century . . . they must depend almost entirely on written sources (and possibly *archaeological evidence*)" (1980, p. xv; emphasis added). Statements demonstrating microhistorians' frequent fascination with archaeology encourage modern-world archaeologists to engage with microhistory, especially since its focus on the minutely local may seem to be at odds with the goals of modern-world archaeology.

SOME ARCHAEOLOGICAL HISTORY

Before we consider microhistory, a brief overview of the concern over scale in archaeology is useful. How one sees the proper scale or frame of archaeological research directly impacts the conception of the micro and whether it should constitute the sole emphasis of research. In Chapter 2 I explored the issue of scale as Braudel and others have considered it. Here I wish to interrogate scale in the abstract to sharpen the connections between modern-world archaeology and microhistory.

Archaeologists, regardless of their era or region of interest, have long pondered their discipline's most appropriate scale of analysis. The urge to move beyond the single site—to broaden the archaeological gaze—was one reason that archaeologists researching pre-1500 societies adopted world-systems analysis in the first place. The application of world-systems analysis was enlightening because it caused archaeologists to ponder several important questions. What level of analysis is most likely to reveal the greatest information about past daily life? Will the most relevant evidence come from the household (the site), the community (several sites), or the region (many more sites)? Confusion about scale is inherent in the nature of archaeological practice because field research necessarily focuses on the minutely local. Archaeologists are renowned for carefully excavating trash pits, cellars, postholes, and living floors—human-built features that may cover less than one-half meter of the earth's surface. The archaeological fascination with such tiny places may make it seem incongruous to speak about global historical archaeology.

What business does an archaeologist have examining any scale larger than a site? If we find a site that once contained 25 houses, all of which have archaeological remains that can be examined, is this not enough to keep an excavator busy for years and perhaps even a lifetime? A related—and perhaps even more cynical—question is "Can archaeologists really offer any information about past social or cultural realities that are not strictly site related?" If these questions are answered in the negative, then modern-world archaeology has no place in historical archaeology. Why should we imagine that an archaeologist's gaze can (or even should) extend beyond the limits of a single site, especially given the added complexities of considering many sites?

Questions such as these, which incorporate making decisions about the "proper" scale of research, bedevil all archaeologists. The historical archaeologist's dilemma about scale may be partially the result of the field's close association with the field of history itself. All historical archaeologists read historians' narratives (secondary accounts developed from primary documents) to develop a basic understanding of the historical context in which their site's inhabitants lived. The work of historians helps archaeologists "get their feet on the ground" (literally) so that they can have some understanding of the conditions their site's inhabitants confronted in their daily lives. This initial reading also helps historical archaeologists become conversant with the relevant historical sources. In a great many cases (and perhaps in all cases), the archaeologist may wish to examine the original primary sources to learn details historians may have missed or judged as unimportant to their narratives.

Such accounts by historians, though profoundly relevant to archaeological research, often have a drawback that involves scale. In writing sweeping accounts, historians must adopt a broad perspective that may encompass a huge territory (an entire nation or continent) or a large segment of time (perhaps an entire century or more). The problem of historical scale is made more complex if the historian's concern is with a transcontinental subject, such as trans-Atlantic migration or culture contact along the coast of the Indian Ocean.

Archaeology and the Problem of Scale

Historical archaeologists have understood the problem of framing for many years. For example, in the 1970s a number of archaeologists indirectly considered the importance of analytical scale by proposing that they worked at the broadest, most profound level possible. As proponents of an explicitly scientific archaeology, they sought to discover general laws of human behavior. This approach drew a distinction between the nomothetic (seeking laws) and the particularistic (or humanistic). Particularistic archaeologists tended to focus on the small and the mundane, seeing their research as more historical than anthropological. Archaeologists with a humanistic bent thought that archaeologists often relied too heavily on scientific explanations and missed the point of historical archaeology: to provide historically rich, thoroughly contextualized examinations of single sites and settlements.

The fundamental difference between the approaches advocated by these two camps was stark. Whereas the archaeologists who saw their research as essentially historical in nature presented deeply detailed, historically rich investigations of one or two sites, the "archaeological scientists" preferred to use several sites in an attempt to identify artifact patterns that reveal broad-scale elements of past cultural behavior.

By the 1980s some archaeologists had begun to argue for an approach that was anthropological in orientation but not focused on the laws of human behavior. In other words, some archaeologists wished to reassert that an important strength of archaeology was precisely its ability to provide exacting, extremely detailed information about single sites, but with the union of anthropological ideas and insights. One such approach within historical archaeology was dubbed "historic ethnography."

For Robert Schuyler writing in 1988, historic ethnography—which he perceived as a phase in the development of a "New Culture History" in historical archaeology—was partly a reaction against the use of world-systems analysis. In his claim that archaeologists "do not excavate on a global level," he urged archaeologists to concentrate their attention on individual sites and communities because these represented the most historically cohesive units of culture. His approach thus advocated a middle ground between the minutely historical world of the humanists and the broadly anthropological world of the scientists. For him site-specific studies could create interpretations that are anthropological *and* historical.

Schuyler's idea is important to note, even though it diverges in important ways from the perspective of modern-world archaeology. First, I would not describe archaeological studies as historic ethnographies. Archaeologists do not have recourse to participant observation, one of the hallmarks of ethnographic fieldwork, so any ethnography created only with archaeological evidence is bound to be incomplete. This is not to say, of course, that archaeologists cannot profitably employ ethnographic information and techniques in their research because they use them all the time.

The principles of modern-world archaeology also reject Schuyler's view that historical archaeologists will always make their greatest contribution at the site level. Site-specific studies are central to providing concrete information about past daily life, but modern-world archaeology posits that the archaeologist's gaze is not required to terminate at the limits of an archaeological site. Archaeological research that is too finely focused has the potential of being relegated to the realm of curiosity, rather than being judged as an important anthropological endeavor capable of explaining how the world we live in came to be.

By the 1990s most historical archaeologists had determined that everyone should solve the problem of scale in his or her own way. As a result some archaeologists have pursued broad-scale studies (but not always employing concepts from world-systems analysis), while others have been content focusing their energies on the historical interpretation of only one or two sites. Each type of analysis, which for the sake of convenience we might term "macro" and "micro" studies respectively, significantly advances the cause of historical archaeology. Each mode of analysis demonstrates the field's interpretive power and adds to our collective cultural knowledge.

Despite the proliferation of scalar studies, however, a central question has remained: can historical archaeologists provide interpretations of modern history's major historical trends and social processes by referring to individual archaeological sites or small collections of sites? This troublesome question poses an especially knotty problem for archaeologists wishing to provide broad-scale analyses of the sort presented by Braudel and Wallerstein. How are archaeologists to address this question since all their field research begins at a concrete—often quite small—place?

Historians interested in local history have also pondered the question of scale. Do local historians writing about small groups of people and their discrete communities have anything pertinent to say to historians working at much larger scales? Can a detailed examination of one small community in Bengal have any relevance to the history of the entire Indian nation since independence? A number of microhistorians, initially intent on the small and the local, seek to address such questions. Since modern-world archaeologists have the same concern, it is important to understand the principal features of microhistory and discover how its strengths and weaknesses can be applied to the archaeological investigation of post-1500 history.

THE ESSENCES OF MICROHISTORY

In 1959 American historian George R. Stewart was one of the first historians to use the term "microhistory" to describe the approach of interpreting history by minutely examining a single past occurrence. The episode he chose was Pickett's charge, a fifteen-hour event that happened on July 3, 1863, during the Battle of Gettysburg.

Stewart's study is a microanalysis in the purest sense of the term, but his larger goal is to demonstrate how this one tiny sequence of actions impacted a significant piece of American history. He believed that historians could use even the smallest of historical events to discover things about the wider processes of human nature. Thinking that warfare represented human nature in its most raw form, he focused on a single attack that occurred within one battle of a continental war that had national and even global significance. As a result his work represents the earliest most extreme form of microhistory, one in which a single infantry charge is linked to the full sweep of human history.

Historians at the time generally ignored Stewart's attempt to write a new kind of historical narrative, and it would be over a decade before other historians would recognize microhistory as a legitimate form of research. Microhistory is now firmly entrenched within the historical mainstream, such that today it would be impossible to enumerate all the microhistorical studies historians have produced over the past ten years.

The abundance of studies that now exist understandably means that variation occurs in how individual historians practice microhistory. They have not created—and indeed probably would not wish to create—a concrete formula historians can universally apply. No one "right" way exists to do microhistory. As is true of all historical writing, each individual practitioner is free to write microhistory according to his or her own personal preferences and theoretical outlook. Nonetheless, historians who have examined the rise and development of microhistory have identified some trends that express the general ways in which their colleagues have approached this form of historical analysis.

Some have likened the practice of microhistory to detective work, stating that their methods approximate those of Sigmund Freud and Sherlock Holmes. Believing trifles—events and things that other investigators might have overlooked or chosen not to consider—to be important, both Freud (in reality) and Holmes (in fiction) minutely examined them. Psychoanalysts, detectives, and microhistorians examine tiny details in their efforts to unravel larger mysteries. (Again, the analogy with archaeology applies because many popular writers regularly describe archaeology as similar to detective work.)

Ginzburg's Microhistory

One of the most iconic microhistoric detective stories is Carlo Ginzburg's account of the life of an obscure sixteenth century miller named Domenico Scandella (called Menocchio), a man who ran afoul of the Inquisition and was subsequently burned at the stake. Ginsburg provided an engaging narrative history of Menocchio's life and troubles and in the process illustrated the interpretive power of microhistory. In addition to describing what he could piece together about the miller's life, Ginzburg also offered rich detail about daily life in one small early modern European town and illustrated how larger forces—such as religious intolerance—affected the lives of ordinary townspeople, including most dramatically Menocchio himself.

Ginzburg used the Italian Inquisition's intense questioning of Menocchio as a way to explore the many tensions that appeared in the sixteenth century as the Italian people experienced large-scale cultural changes. One significant change that had an immediate and devastating affect on Menocchio was the clash between time-honored oral traditions and the newly available printed word. As an autodidact and avid reader, Menocchio was conflicted about some of what he read, and his apparent willingness to communicate his new philosophical questions to his unlettered neighbors helped convince his Inquisitors that he was a dangerous heretic who deserved to be silenced.

To create the context of the miller's daily life, Ginzburg outlined the network relations in which Menocchio operated. At a larger scale, however, he also documented how the transition between medieval and post-medieval worlds filtered down to and impacted the miller's everyday existence. Part of the transition involved the evolving class structure of the post-medieval era. During this period of history, conflict was developing between the dominant (literate) class and the subordinate (illiterate) classes—a divide Menocchio crossed much to his detriment.

Ginzburg's interest in connecting the micro (one obscure miller's heretofore forgotten life) and the macro (larger issues within early modern European life lived under the scrutinizing and unsympathetic eyes of the Inquisition) demonstrated an important goal of microhistorical research. Using analogies with anthropological fieldwork, Ginzburg sought in each of his studies to compile ethnographies of everyday life by reference to small social units: an individual, a single family, a lone community or village. This goal is familiar to traditional historical archaeologists as historic ethnography, but Ginzburg's study of Menocchio's life and times highlighted two strengths of microhistory pertinent to modern-world archaeology: the focus on history's forgotten, overlooked, and denigrated people, and the importance of recognizing social networks. These elements reach beyond the goals of historic ethnography.

Microhistory and the Lower Orders

One of the features of microhistory immediately apparent in Ginzburg's study is that this kind of history often focuses on people who once inhabited the lower orders of society. Microhistory thus constitutes a form of "history from below," narratives written about people who were not born to privilege and about which little might actually be known. Readers familiar with the history of historical archaeology will recognize that the term "inarticulate" (used in the late 1960s and early 1970s) is consistent with the concept of history from below. Like much historical archaeology, microhistories are also known for uncovering and interpreting elements of past popular culture that are now long forgotten. Some of these practices, hidden from view at the time they were conducted, can only be revealed through careful analysis. Historical archaeologists will see corollaries in research carried out on past magical practices, such as the creation of witch bottles in Britain and the African-American custom of hiding spirit bundles in buildings and yards.

The microhistorians' focus on "commoners" has at least two significant similarities with contemporary historical archaeology. The first similarity involves a concern for providing unique information about peoples who are poorly known from historical documents, or who have been portrayed unfairly or not at all. Many historical archaeologists, stretching back to the very beginning of the field's professionalization in the late 1960s, have been especially concerned with pursuing the same kind of research. A second similarity between much historical archaeology and microhistory involves illuminating the roles common people like Menocchio played in the creation of large-scale history. This overt multiscalar approach means that microhistorical analysis is especially relevant to modern-world archaeology.

Microhistorical studies of poorly known peoples indicate how the local creates the global in decidedly human terms. Microhistorians refer to this approach as the "exceptional-normal." In exceptional-normal narratives, the authors concentrate on an unusual event—rather than on larger social processes—as their starting point. They then use this starting point as a base from which to delve deeper into local history and to disentangle the complex web of local : global connections that affected the individual or group that constitutes the focus of study.

Ginzburg's careful narration of Menocchio's torture at the hands of the Italian Inquisition is a prominent and especially evocative example of this approach. Menocchio's situation was completely unique because he was a commoner who learned to read and thus ponder profound issues that the elites assumed were beyond his "station." Yet his situation was also simultaneously somewhat typical because he was not the only person who ran afoul of the Inquisition. His story, though terribly unique at one scale (the individual), was completely common at another (the collective). Understanding the dialectics of his position is consistent with the core values of modern-world archaeology.

Microhistory and Colonial America

Another excellent example of an exceptional-normal case study appears in Donna Merwick's *Death of a Notary: Conquest and Change in Colonial New York*. This account is worth considering because readers outside the history profession are less familiar with it. Like Ginzburg's study of Menocchio, however, it provides a superb case study with important lessons for modern-world archaeology.

Merwick began at the smallest level of analysis possible: a lone individual on a single day in the past. Her subject is the life and death of a man named Adriaen Janse van Ilpendam and the date is March 12, 1686. The exceptionality of the case derived from Janse being the only person in seventeenth century Albany, New York (then a Dutch colony), to have committed suicide. Of all the people who lived in that colonial outpost for decades, he was the only person before 1686 to decide to end his own life. In this respect Janse was completely exceptional. Given this special circumstance, how "normal" was his life? In other words, how can such a unique narrative reflect anything for a broader scale of analysis? Merwick provided answers that are enlightening and useful.

Janse's lifetime occurred during a truly transformative era in colonial American and indeed global history. For most of his life he lived in a place called New Netherland, but at the end of his life he was a resident of New York—even though he had not moved. The place had changed around him. From the founding of New Netherland at Fort Orange in 1624 until 1664, the Hudson River valley (the site of Albany) was in possession of the Dutch United Provinces. The cultural traditions practiced by Janse and his neighbors were Dutch and their maritime connections were mostly with Amsterdam and Rotterdam. But in 1664 an English fleet sailed into Manhattan harbor and took possession of the city of New Amsterdam. The newcomers promptly renamed the city New York after the Duke of York. With the signing of the Treaty of Breda three years later, the Dutch government formally surrendered its claim to what it still called New Netherland.

During the Third Anglo-Dutch War of 1673, however, the Dutch retook the city and renamed it New Orange. They also promptly reestablished their Dutch administrative procedures and recommenced life as they had formerly known it. But their new administration lasted only about fourteen months. With the Treaty of Westminster, signed far away from the town of New Orange, the Dutch finally lost their claim to New York. Each of these important geopolitical transactions took place a long distance from Janse's home, but each one was to have a profound affect upon him.

Janse's life story, though entirely unique and personal, cannot be separated from the rhythms of conflict between the powerful Dutch and English empires. His career as a notary placed him directly within this global maelstrom precisely because he made his living writing legal papers. The national traditions of the colony's political leadership had a powerful impact on all aspects of the legal profession, including upon those individuals who transcribed the colony's legal writs and contracts. And in 1674 English Governor Edmund Andros, soon after his arrival in New York City, mandated that the colony would conduct all its business according to English standards.

This requirement meant that all legal proceedings had to be performed according to English common law and that all documents must be written in English rather than Dutch. This change profoundly affected Janse because not only was he required to become conversant with an unfamiliar language and legal system, but he also had to make an adjustment about time itself. As a Dutchman Janse was comfortable dating his documents using the Gregorian calendar, but since the English used the Julian calendar, he had to learn (and remember) to use this format in his official documents. But uncertain times led to uncertain actions and Janse was often confused about what place name to put on his documents. Did he live in Fort Orange (the first permanent Dutch fortification), Beverwijck (the fur-trading town that had grown up north of the fort), Willemstadt (the town's most recent Dutch name), or New Albany in America (the most recent English name)? The troublesome tension between the familiar Dutch practices and those of the novel English is amply demonstrated by one simple act performed after Janse's death: the English scribe listed his name as "Adriaen *Johnson* van Elpendam." So in the end the Dutchman Janse effectively became the Englishman Johnson, a final transformation.

Each of the decisions Janse was called upon to make involved a complex arrangement of scales because the local was constantly colliding against and blending with the global, just as the global was endlessly impinging upon the local. Janse and the other Dutch men and women who lived along the banks of the Hudson River faced daily humiliation as they lost their "cultural fluency." They had to conduct business in an English city using English conventions. All legal records had to be written in the English language. As a result, as Merwick says, "Janse's life was inescapably entangled with the English conquest of New Netherland" (1999, p. 186). He had to become as English as he could to keep his business flowing; he had to learn and adapt to a new, imposed epochal substructure. This legal substructure, because it existed within Eurocentrism, demonstrates that different nation-states can express Eurocentrism differently—at times even violently, as in the case of war. Paradoxically, however, Janse had to be careful that he not appear to have become so English that he alienated his many Dutch clients. One never knew if the Dutch masters would one day return again to New York. His cultural confusion was not his alone, however. Every Dutch person in Albany undoubtedly experienced this double consciousness to varying degrees, but Janse sought escape through suicide.

Merwick's analysis, though dedicated to the exceptional-normal approach, prompts a question. Would it be possible to conceptualize Janse's complex life without understanding the context that was framed by the wider universe of European intercultural contact and conflict? The reality of his life story aptly demonstrates that external factors can affect events and processes that, without introspection, may at first seem completely local.

Microhistory and the Importance of Social Networks

One of the microhistorian's goals is to correct the traditional historian's overemphasis on political and legal history by focusing on social networks and cultural variables. Microhistorians seek to uncover and investigate social interactions that occurred between real historical individuals, rather than to perceive these historical actors as mere analytical categories. Their narratives, like those of Merwick and Ginzburg, reveal the social networks within which real people in the past lived. This goal is completely consistent with modern-world archaeology. As noted above, modern-world archaeology posits that archaeologists must consider social networks at all times, even when interpreting single sites. Janse's story helps us understand the need for this kind of analysis.

Microhistorians affirm the central importance of social relations. For Ginzburg's Menocchio a relevant network is composed of his fellow villagers. These were the people with whom he questioned the true nature of God and these were the people who led the Inquisition directly to him. The extant documents contain many of these individuals' names, though we know little about them or the precise nature of his conversations with them. The outcome, however, tells us that he must have shocked and worried them. For Janse the colonial residents seeking his expertise as a notary—as well as his neighbors—constituted one level of his network relations. But Janse, like Menocchio, also lived within larger webs of association that extended far beyond any one place. After the English took control of New Amsterdam, Janse discovered that what happened thousands of miles away had a direct and immediate bearing upon his daily life and livelihood. He learned that he was enmeshed in trans-Atlantic networks that were as real as the many local networks involving his face-to-face contacts with neighbors and clients.

Network theory teaches that any particular web of interaction can have multiple dimensions that stretch horizontally through space and vertically through time (see Chapter 3). Given this knowledge, a major issue for microhistorians to resolve is how to define the boundaries of the networks. In other words, how do microhistorians decide the size of their frame of reference? When does the micro become the macro?

Multiple analytical scales may encourage different interpretations, because what is seen one way in a narrow frame may appear dissimilar (and perhaps even unfamiliar) in a broader frame. Modern-world archaeology does not seek to decide the "proper" level of analysis that will fit all archaeological analysis; lived experience is much too socially complex and historically variable to permit analytical rigidity. Like microhistorians, each archaeologist must decide the analytical framework that best conforms to the needs of his or her research design. The key for modern-world archaeology is that every analysis, even the most site-specific examples, should contain an acknowledgment of the broader social networks within which real people lived. The goals of modern-world archaeology are not served by site-specific studies having no wider implications than the boundaries of the site itself. Even so, modern-world archaeologists do use particularistic studies to create broader analyses, but the effectiveness of these investigations will depend upon the quality of the original study.

DOES MICROANALYSIS CONTAIN ANY DANGERS FOR HISTORICAL ARCHAEOLOGY?

Like particularistic historical archaeology, microhistory has had its critics. The most frequently cited pitfall is inherent within its very focus, because microhistory can be assailed as mere antiquarianism. Microhistorians can concentrate so intently on the minute that they may overlook the larger issues; their narratives can be completely focused on the narrowest frame to the exclusion of all else.

Part of the problem arises from the exceptional-normal approach itself. The accounts offered by microhistorians, exemplified by the sad tales of Menocchio and Janse, typically present historical individuals who had something unusual happen to them that is worth recounting. Menocchio confronted the Italian Inquisition with his doubts about the logical nature of Christianity and Janse was the only person in the entire history of Dutch New Netherland to commit suicide. The exceptional qualities of their life histories can make it difficult to substantiate the relevance of their personal stories to their contemporary societies at large. One obvious solution is threefold: the historian should remain focused on the social networks, seek to understand how they change or persist over time, and demonstrate how some personal histories extend far beyond the individual's daily orbit of contacts. Modern-world archaeologists remember at all times that social networks extend through time and space in complex, multifaceted ways, and that networks are simultaneously horizontal and vertical.

Overly particularistic historical archaeology runs the same risks as microhistory. One of the formidable dangers of a too finely tuned archaeological study is that it can be easy for the public to dismiss it as irrelevant. A taxpaying citizen may wonder why professors at a state university spend their time measuring pipestem bore sizes and writing articles about buttons. This situation is not difficult to imagine. Such ideas offer commentary on the contemporary union of anti-intellectualism and the need for practicality in capitalism. Students are encouraged to enroll in educational programs designed to lead to high-paying careers, rather than to follow their interests.

The economic reality here reflects how the global affects the local, as the world's economic crises impact a society's perception of what constitutes "important" research. Minutely focused studies on pipestem bore diameters, transfer-printed ceramic colors, and the shapes of trade kettles constitute basic material culture research. Archaeologists should never abandon these kinds of analyses, nor would many ever wish to do so. The activities of careful researchers, so often misunderstood by the public, allow archaeological knowledge to advance. This work also provides much of the basic information for modern-world archaeology.

At the same time, however, one of the key tenets of modern-world archaeology is that archaeology can never be just about the minute and the detailed. Archaeologists have a responsibility to provide information about the materiality of past daily life and historical archaeologists have a particular responsibility in this regard. The material and social realities of the rise of the capitalist project, the invasions of colonialists, the ideologies of Eurocentrists, and the perniciousness of those advancing racialized hierarchies demand to be told from an archaeological standpoint. Modern-world archaeology unapologetically has the telling of these histories as one of its most important goals.

Another pitfall of purely particularistic historical archaeology is that it denies the significance of socially responsible archaeology. Increasing numbers of archaeologists have recently come to realize the power of their discipline to contribute to the societal conceptualization and comprehension of contemporary life. A growing number of practicing archaeologists now recognize the importance of making overt linkages between the present and the past. Younger practitioners should realize that this was not always true. Archaeologists now readily admit that their research has the power to illuminate contemporary problems including waste disposal, overcrowding, and environmental degradation. I explore some of these ideas in Chapter 7, but here I simply wish to note that historical archaeology—because its subject matter is so close to our own time, and in fact sometimes actually focuses on our time—is especially well suited to providing knowledge that is readily applicable to today's social and environmental contexts. And it is here again that we can see the importance of analyzing the "four haunts" of the modern world with archaeological information. This, then, comes back to the subject of microhistory.

Without question the small worlds of everyday life retain myriad connections with the larger worlds dominated by political and socioeconomic practices, ideologies, and structures. Both microhistory and microhistorical archaeology have an incredible potential to enlighten us about the small worlds of individuals like Menocchio and Janse (and other actors rescued from the obscurity of history), but such minute stories should not be the end point of archaeological research. Modern-world archaeology challenges archaeologists to use their considerable interpretive skills to address how obscure individuals—people so much like us in myriad ways—manipulated, struggled against, accommodated, and used the epochal structures within which they found themselves. It was within these tiny spaces, these myriad horizontal and vertical social and physical networks, that individuals of the past—just like individuals alive today—created their daily lives.

SUGGESTED READINGS

Ginzburg, Carlo. 1980. *The Cheese and the Worms: The Cosmos of a Sixteenth-Century Miller*. Translated by John Tedeschi and Anne C. Tedeschi. Johns Hopkins University Press, Baltimore, MD.
  One of the most well-known and fun-to-read microhistories available.

Magnússon, Sigurthur G. 2003. "The Singularization of History": Social History and Microhistory Within the Postmodern State of Knowledge. *Journal of Social History* 36:701–735.
  A scholarly consideration of microhistory as a kind of social history. Difficult but important.

Merwick, Donna. 1999. *Death of a Notary: Conquest and Change in Colonial New York*. Cornell University Press, Ithaca, NY.
  The microhistory of Janse in New Netherland. A wonderful case study of the interconnections between the local and the global.

Schuyler, Robert L. 1988. Archaeological Remains, Documents, and Anthropology: A Call for a New Culture History. *Historical Archaeology* 22:36–42.
  Presents the definition of historic ethnography and argues for its relevance. Useful to compare with microhistory.

Stewart, George R. 1959. *Pickett's Charge: A Microhistory of the Final Attack at Gettysburg, July 3, 1863*. Houghton Mifflin, Boston.
  An early microhistory demonstrating how the very small can be connected to much larger historical events and processes.

STUDY QUESTIONS

1. Give reasons why so many microhistorians refer to their research as archaeological when they do not conduct excavations.

2. Explain some of the similarities between Ginzburg's and Merwick's methods.

3. State three reasons why microhistorical archaeology is important.

4. State three reasons why archaeologists should not end their analyses at the micro level.

CHAPTER 6

ARTIFACTS

None of what I have written about in the preceding chapters would be possible without the tangible remains of past human activity. Here, then, we must turn to a consideration of artifacts—the most basic and unique source of information available to modern-world archaeologists (Figure 9).

To write about artifacts in archaeology is to enter a tangled web of theories, counter-theories, hypotheses, and counter-hypotheses. Archaeologists often treat theories of material culture like they would a bowl of candy. They search through it looking for a particular piece that looks appealing at the time, and once selected they enjoy it for awhile. Before long, however, they finish it and move on to a new piece. They may choose a completely different piece and enjoy this one for awhile, never thinking back to the first one they enjoyed. Or if they think about the first piece at all, they often react with disdain and eagerly explain—frequently in the harshest terms—how misguided their selection process was in the past. In some cases they may condemn the choices of others, too.

The question of how archaeologists select their interpretations is difficult to answer. In some instances their choice may be based solely upon newness and popularity; many people may be drawn to an idea simply because of its novelty. An interpretation with an unfamiliar lexicon may seem to offer insights never before imagined. One of the troubling aspects of archaeological theory is that many archaeologists may discard perfectly sound interpretive frameworks long before they have had the opportunity to explore all their implications and potential. In far too many cases, good ideas are rapidly abandoned in favor of the new. The cavalier dismissal of good ideas before they are fully investigated ultimately harms the advance of theory development in archaeology.

Figure 9. Excavation of a white clay smoking pipe, originally a commodity.

ARCHAEOLOGY'S ENCHANTMENT WITH OBJECTS

Without question the ways in which archaeologists interpret objects from the past has changed over time. What was once the leading edge of archaeological thought begins to appear outdated. Terms such as "sociotechnic" and "ideotechnic," exciting and promising in the late 1960s, now seem too simple. Theories come and go with regularity and progress is slowly made.

The newest artifact-related idea today is contained within a poorly conceptualized perspective called thing theory. The newness of this lexicon promises to provide a glut of archaeological studies, even though the ideas seem more suited to scholars who have just discovered artifact analysis and interpretation rather than to seasoned archaeologists. Archaeologists have long considered just about everything included in thing theory, and the ideas of thing theorists—when viewed dispassionately without regard to their novelty—seem to offer little that is new or enlightening. Thing theory appears naive compared with recent ideas presented by archaeologists investigating the connections among peoples, ideas, and things.

Even the briefest survey of archaeological history demonstrates that the field has always been dedicated to understanding what is now being grandly termed "human-thing entanglement" (itself an example of a new term for an old idea). Scholars in other disciplines have also begun to think about artifacts. Historians, for example, have recently rediscovered the material world and have sought to wrest the study of objects away from the social sciences. And sociologists, not wishing to be left behind, are also proclaiming their interest in materiality. So pervasive is this "discovery" that even some archaeologists have oddly voiced a need to "return to things." Such "discoveries" evoke smiles among archaeologists who have never stopped thinking that their discipline is about humanity's connection with the material world. Faced with a new terminology—and nonarchaeologists' willingness to appropriate things, just as they have the concept of culture—archaeologists seem to have reached the point where they must proclaim their overt interest in material objects and even defend this interest. This turn of events is indeed a surprising development in the history of archaeological thought!

Rather than entering the convoluted debate over the meaning of artifacts in the abstract, in this chapter I explore the core tenets of artifact analysis and interpretation relevant to modern-world archaeology. My goal is not to rummage through the existing bowl of theories, seeking to discover a stunningly new one that will hopefully provide startling new views of the world. Nor do I intend to adopt a new set of terms to account for old concepts, seeking merely to make long-agreed-upon ideas seem fresh and innovative simply by packaging them differently. Rather, my goal is to return to some of the foundational ideas of artifact interpretation in modern-world archaeology and relate this to artifact analysis in historical archaeology.

Artifacts as Relational Objects

Modern-world archaeology is best served by concentrating first and foremost on the understanding that artifacts are inherently relational objects. Modern-world archaeology is relational to its core and it is from this angle that the artifacts of the modern world are best approached. The points I wish to reaffirm are:

- All artifacts, regardless of date, mediate human relationships; artifacts, like people, are enmeshed in networks of interaction.
- Most of the artifacts of the modern world have an initial meaning that is distinct from those produced and used before 1500.
- As indicated in Figure 10, the vast majority of post-1500 artifacts were originally created as commodities (and increasingly so as we approach our own time).
- Commodities, because of their very reason for being, mediate economic relationships as their initial function.
- All noneconomic relationships that work through physical things develop only after they have been imbued with new

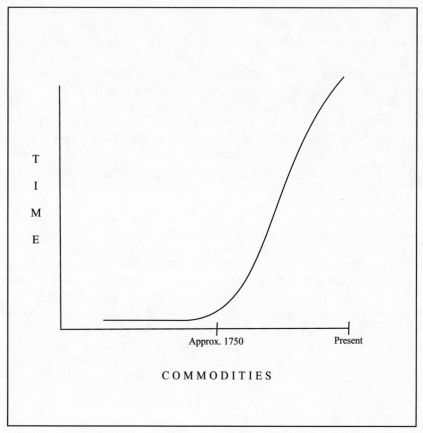

Figure 10. Simplified model of the worldwide increase in commodities through time.

meanings—or, in other words, after they have ceased to function purely as commodities.
• Taste, added to economics, explains why people surround themselves with certain collections of material culture.

This approach permits modern-world archaeologists to appreciate the role physical objects play in the post-1500 world and to understand the diverse ways they create, maintain, and reinforce social relations among individuals and between them and their environments. This understanding also allows us to acknowledge artifacts' social elements without having to rely on social theories that downplay or undermine the role of economics in modern life.

Archaeologists today understand the universality of the human : artifact relation, a perspective relevant at the largest scale possible. The internal wisdom of this insight—when viewed at the scale of pan-human experience—conforms to general anthropological thinking. Artifacts have mediated between humans and their diverse environments since the first hominid picked up a rock and used it to crack open a shell. Quite simply, human life without artifacts is impossible.

Most practicing archaeologists now accept that artifacts, though inanimate, play significant and active—albeit diverse—roles in at least five relationships: between individuals, between individuals and groups, between groups, between individuals and their environment, and between groups and their environment. The goal of archaeological analysis is to devise ways to interpret the various meanings conveyed by the artifacts enmeshed within these relationships. Numerous empirical studies demonstrate that humans often recontextualize artifacts to the point that their actual, in-the-world meanings are quite distinct from what the artifacts' producers originally planned or perhaps even imagined. Modern-world archaeology, though focused initially on the commoditization of artifacts in the post-1500 world, never forgets the significance of recontextualization throughout an artifact's life history.

Modern-world archaeology assumes that the rudimentary feature of most post-1500 artifacts is that they began life as commodities. In this role the commodity expresses its relationship to one of the central hallmarks of modernity: the rise of global mercantilism and capitalism. Commodities rest deep within the rationale of the marketplace because without them the large-scale, truly global commerce of the post-1500 world would have been impossible.

The connection between modernity and commodities is not to suggest, of course, that exchangeable goods were not present in the world before the birth of the mercantilist mindset. Archaeologists of antiquity regularly discover trade goods during their excavations. Many of these, such as the copper daggers related to the Bell Beaker phenomenon of Europe's third millennium BCE or the artifacts Frank used to make his case for his version of the world system (see Chapter 2), have indeed traveled long distances from their point of origin to their place of deposit. Nonetheless, as a purely theoretical matter we suggest that pre-1500 and post-1500 objects of exchange were distinct—even though at the broadest scale they share many characteristics. The difference between them requires explanation.

THE DISTINCTION OF MODERN–WORLD ARTIFACTS

Modern-world archaeology has as a central understanding that the objects used in the modern era were metaphysically different, at least in one sense, from those created in pre-modern times. This is a controversial issue in archaeological circles, especially among archaeologists who insist that historical archaeology is no different from prehistoric archaeology. I have long argued for a distinction between the two archaeologies, mainly because of the inherent difference in the genealogy of the respective material cultures when viewed holistically. Put straightforwardly, most artifacts made and used in 1770 CE had a different initial meaning from those made and used in 1770 BCE. One of the key elements of this distinction is that artifacts made in 1770 CE share many of the same characteristics as artifacts made and used today. This similarity means that archaeologists of the modern world can use artifacts to explore issues that have direct present-day relevance.

Some of the research questions posed in modern-world archaeology may be completely irrelevant to pre-modern history. We can witness the difficulty of attempting to apply modern-world circumstances to prehistoric situations simply by recalling the problems ancient Near Eastern and pre-Columbian Mesoamerican archaeologists have had trying to apply Wallerstein's world-systems analysis to their archaeological contexts. Archaeologists in these cases have generally found the theory wanting and have rejected it. Their failure to find Wallerstein's ideas useful is not surprising because he specifically developed world-systems analysis to account for modern-era global history, not to explain the entire history of exchange (see Chapter 2).

Racialization and Access to Material Things

Another good example derives from considering the relationships between racialization and material access. We know today that ancient individuals who controlled social power and had society-wide authority often classified disparate peoples as inferior. The unequal power structure had the practical result that those judged inferior had little access to certain classes of material culture. Archaeologists of ancient history have successfully investigated this kind of social inequality using the remains of tombs from cultures as diverse as the Maya and the ancient Egyptians. These efforts are important but modern-world archaeologists can often reach deeper understandings of human : artifact relations because of the greater number of source materials available to them.

But even in more recently dated cases where a paucity of information exists, the greatest difference between the research of modern-world archaeologists and that of archaeologists studying earlier eras is that the research findings of the former are usually applicable to the world today. The connection between the past and present is more immediate in modern-world archaeology than for earlier archaeologies. I am not suggesting that pre-1500 archaeology is unimportant; quite the contrary, I am simply saying that archaeologists find it much more difficult to relate their pre-1500 research to the social conditions we face in the world today. We can much more easily relate the conditions of present-day Egyptian society with the events of nineteenth century colonial history than with the circumstances people faced during the Middle Kingdom (ca. 2040–1780 BCE).

Again, this is not to argue that the findings of archaeologists of ancient history are less important than those dealing with the recent past. Such a conclusion would be untrue and unfair. As a purely practical matter, the public continues to be fascinated with all things concerning ancient Egypt, and this interest is good for archaeology in general. But the research of pre-modern archaeologists, though equally valid by all possible measures of scholarship, is not as relevant to present-day life as modern-world archaeology. It remains indisputably true, however, that pre-1500 research adds immeasurably to our collective knowledge about the history of the human condition, but modern-world archaeology is by definition intimately connected with our own time and its researches cannot be divorced from it.

To begin to appreciate the important distinction between pre-modern and modern-period artifacts, we can briefly contemplate the birth of artifacts in both eras. This initial exploration, though purely hypothetical, helps sharpen our point of view. In pre-modern times—and increasingly so, as one moves backward in time from about 1500—the users of most objects were also most likely their producers or were individuals within relatively close trading distance. In the modern era—and increasingly so, as we move closer to our own time from 1500—the residents of a family home did not make their own material things; they purchased them in greater numbers as we move closer to the present. People living in capitalist environments today buy just about everything they own. Even a person knitting a scarf, brewing beer in the basement, or cooking gourmet meals must purchase the wool, the equipment, and the pots. Of course this neat scenario is not completely true because of the existence of pre-1500 trading networks, but it has the most illustrative power if we envision tribal versus industrial societies as polar opposites for the purpose of explanation. Our particular interest rests in the relations of production within each type of society.

The Role of Production

The production of pottery provides an excellent example. Craft potters living in tribal societies fashioned their vessels from local clays using the traditional methods older craftspersons had taught them. Many—and perhaps all—of their teachers might be related to the students through networks of descent or marriage. Potters were able to introduce or modify decorative styles because of internal social changes or contacts with foreigners. Potters also could put culturally significant symbols on the vessels they fashioned, elements that would convey special meanings to everyone who saw them. If they wished, they could also add purely idiosyncratic designs.

By contrast, the situation in the modern era is quite different. With the rise of mercantilism and then capitalism, pottery—now glazed ceramics— was increasingly produced in factory environments by wage-earning laborers. These workers had far less emotional connection to the pieces they produced and they were not at liberty to apply symbols and decorations of their own choosing; decorative elements were imposed from above by foremen who passed along the instructions they received from the factory owners. This design process became increasingly standardized as capitalist production matured, even though some personal creativity was occasionally possible.

The production process in both cases may well reflect what some economists have termed "producer sovereignty," but in distinctly different ways. When factory production of glazed ceramics was just beginning, individual folk potters working outside the factory system could still apply culturally meaningful decorative elements to the vessels they personally made; in the factory model, ceramic decorators had no control over what they could put on a vessel's surface (with the exception of an occasional personal mark slipped in on the bottom of a factory-made piece).

This simplified example of production is easy to conceptualize but real life is seldom so straightforward. Nonetheless, the basic distinction between the productive processes in the two situations holds true. The key aspect of the example is that the ceramics produced in the modern factory are true commodities because they are created with the purpose of being exchanged for something else of value. The vessels produced in the tribal example may have been used in trade, but this usage was not necessary. The distinction is important because the rise of commoditization is a key feature of post-1500 history.

Commoditization constitutes an important subject for modern-world archaeology and is a topic that is particularly suitable to archaeological analysis. The prominence of commodities in today's globalized world perfectly substantiates the need for archaeological analysis. As a result modern-world historical archaeologists must understand the qualities and complexities of commodities.

THE NATURE OF COMMODITIES

Commodities are not unique to the modern era. The beginnings of trade are deeply buried in humanity's past. Residents of the ancient cities that stretched out along the coasts of present-day Lebanon and Syria relied on long-distance trade for decades, and a commercial class developed there as long ago as the tenth century BCE. The same developments occurred in the eastern coastal areas of the Yellow Sea during the 500 BCE–500 CE era as an extensive trading network linked together peoples in today's China, Korea, and Japan. Commodities such as obsidian, gold, amber, and faience circulated throughout prehistoric Europe long before the most incipient mercantilism had ever been imagined, and in central North America—during the first centuries CE—exotic goods regularly moved hundreds of miles. This collective body of archaeological evidence proves that it would be naive to associate commoditization exclusively with the modern era. Many ancient peoples manufactured and exchanged commodities for centuries, so what is unique about the modern era?

This is not the place to argue for the uniqueness of modernity over the rest of human history. Suffice it to say that as far as commodities are concerned, an important distinction between post-1500 history and earlier times relates to two central factors: the geographical spread of a commodity's distribution, and the widespread cultural availability of non-luxury items.

Before 1500 the few commodities that moved around generally traveled either within a single continent or between adjacent continents or regions. Pre-1500 commodities were not moved around the entire world as they were after about 1500 (and increasingly so). In addition, most of the pre-1500 commodities received in trade were specifically intended for elites and so were considered luxury items. One goal of post-1500 mercantilism/ capitalism has been to flood the market with commodities, create demand by stressing personal satisfaction, and sell as much as possible to as many people as possible regardless of their social position. The deceptive complexity of commodities has meant that many social philosophers have accorded them abundant consideration. Their inherent intricacies caused Marx to refer to commodities as "mysterious," "queer" things that have "metaphysical subtleties and theological niceties" (1967 [1867], Vol. I, p. 71).

However we might wish to think about commodities in a philosophical sense, the basic quality to remember is that commodities are a physical embodiment of relations. A commodity links individuals together in interesting, diverse, and socially charged ways. An artifact that is not a commodity does not necessarily have the same relational power as a commodity. An artifact can be made, used, worn out, and discarded without ever having linked its owner to another individual. But all artifacts connect their users to their natural environments. A stone axe, for example, may link an individual to the forest (creating a human : environment connection), but if the axe is not intended specifically for exchange, it is not relational in human : human terms. A commodity requires at least two individuals: an owner who trades it and a consumer who acquires it. A commodity is thus the quintessential relational artifact.

Thinkers like Adam Smith understood that commodities had developed during the creation of divisions of labor. Societal segmentation based on work allowed the rise of a trading class whose members specialized in exchange. Thus a butcher with more meat than his family could consume would look for a way to get rid of the surplus (which was commoditized—

i.e., given a price for sale). To make this rather straightforward transaction, though, the butcher (acting as a part-time member of the trading class) requires two things: someone who wants the surplus meat and a predetermined medium of exchange. It is this second element that introduces further complexity into commodities, because it means that value must be imported to the things that are scheduled for exchange. The person seeking to acquire the butcher's excess meat must have something of equal or greater value to trade for it. The human relations established by trade lead directly to the meaning of value.

VALUE

The concept of value is surprisingly complex. The root cause of the complication rests in the concept that a commodity's value can be expressed in something else; it cannot be expressed in its own terms. One bull can be exchanged for another deemed of equal value but a bull cannot be exchanged for itself. In Volume I of *The Wealth of Nations*, Smith neatly summarized the mutability of exchangeable commodities (as well as the significance of the sociohistorical context).

> The armour of Diomede, says Homer, cost only nine oxen; but that of Glaucus cost an hundred oxen. Salt is said to be the common instrument of commerce and exchanges in Abyssinia; a species of shells in some parts of the coast of India; dried cod at Newfoundland; tobacco in Virginia; sugar in some of our West India colonies; hides or dressed leather in some other countries; and there is at this day a village in Scotland where it is not uncommon, I am told, for a workman to carry nails instead of money to the baker's shop or the ale-house. (1999 [1776], Vol. I, p. 127)

The problem, as Smith showed, is that a medium of exchange must be invented to make the equation of one commodity compatible with another. As Marx observed, twenty yards of linen cannot be valued against twenty yards of the exact same linen. Another entity must stand in for the linen in such a way that its value can be fairly determined, such as nails for currency in Smith's example. Eighteenth century French fur traders in North America set the value of a pile of glass beads or a woolen blanket as equal to a certain number of beaver pelts, just as Smith's ancient traders understood the equivalence between oxen and armor.

The institution of a truly international trade—as commerce linking together wildly diverse cultures—required something to stand in for value. Ancient traders used precious metals (raw or coins) as an early and long-lasting standard measure of exchange. People living in today's market-based societies fully understand and readily accept that the price of a commodity is expressed in terms of dollars, Euros, pesos, and other currencies. But not all value is expressed in the "money-form." A great many objects, once they have been transformed beyond their lives as commodities, have been assigned additional kinds of value.

Kinds of Value

Scholars have long disagreed about how objects contain or exemplify value. Smith, for example, thought that the exchange value of an object (its price in a capitalist setting) was determined by the "toil and trouble of acquiring it." Marx, on the other hand, believed that a commodity's value resided in the amount of labor required to produce it. Despite such disagreements, all philosophers of commodities agree that physical things intended for trade have at least two values: a "value in use" and a "value in exchange." Value in use refers to an artifact's utility, or what it can be made to do. A pair of scissors has the use-value of being able to cut cloth, paper, and other materials. Exchange-value is simply the ability of an artifact to command a certain amount of something else in trade. An ice cream bar has an exchange-value of about $3.00 in the United States. Its "use" is to satisfy the need for something tasty.

Exchange-value and use-value, however, are not always compatible. An object having substantial use may have little exchange-value. A ratty—but intensely comfortable—reading chair may be worth little as an object of exchange, but its use-value may be unlimited to the person who finds solace while sitting in it. Something with great exchange-value may have little or no practical use-value. A diamond ring can have great exchange-value but no practical use. Its non-exchange value may derive from a third kind of value, variously termed "sign," "aesthetic," or "esteem" value.

Theorists view esteem-value as an individual's perception of the commodity or the feelings and emotions it may evoke. This sense of value frequently accounts for the often-obsessive desire to obtain goods in our present-day, hyperconsumerist society. A diamond ring, being devoid of use-value, has profound esteem-value when used to signify commitment and marriage. Over time, should the marriage be successful, it may be that the ring's original exchange-value will be entirely forgotten as its esteem-value increases. If the ring is passed on to a daughter, the exchange-value may no longer be considered unless the ring is pawned or sold. If not sold but cherished, the ring's esteem-value will increase as it grows older; it acquires what is often termed "patina." (If the daughter finds herself in hard times and pawns the ring, it begins life anew as a commodity with exchange-value.)

The important point is that as far as commodities are concerned, exchange-value comes first as a relational quality. Even while a commodity is functioning as an exchange-value, it remains possible (and indeed perhaps even likely) that the consumer wishing to obtain it evaluates its use- and/or esteem-value simultaneously with its price. An eighteenth century First Nations trader may see great practical use in a steel axe, but he may also envision the envy the axe might arouse among his kin group (either positively or negatively). To obtain the axe, the trader must first enter into an exchange relationship with the owner of the axe. The object serves as the intermediary because exchange is not possible without it. This particular trader and the person with the axe might never have had reason to meet without the axe being present. Modern-world archaeologists cannot overlook the relational connection created by the axe or the key role it plays in forging human relationships and complex networks.

A great many historical archaeologists, in searching for symbolic or other interpretations, often overlook the importance of the first relational feature of all the commodities they discover in their excavations. Overlooking these associations does not make them disappear; it simply pushes them into the background. But disregarding this initial relational quality of the artifact-as-commodity means that an important early phase of an artifact's life history is undervalued. Also, ignoring the simple exchangeability of commodities means that attention is drawn away from an additional feature of a commodity's history: its relationships with other commodities with which it shares a life history. These are the social and cultural associations experienced by all commodities as they are transformed by human practice from having only exchange-value to being imbued with use- and esteem-value.

THE SOCIAL IMPERATIVES OF
ARTIFACTS–AS–COMMODITIES

One of the key elements of modern-world archaeology, as noted throughout this book, is that it relies on the concept of interconnectedness. Modern-world archaeology cannot be conducted in the absence of a network consciousness. Thus an archaeologist's avoidance of a commodity's exchange-value misses an important piece of the interpretive puzzle by obscuring an artifact's many relations with other artifacts. All professionally responsible archaeologists are extremely sensitive to the significance of context as a physical fact, but many may not always recognize another sense of the word "context." Simply put, commodities—just like all artifacts—do not exist in a world of their own. They inhabit networks that extend through time and across space. An archaeologist must only contemplate an arrowhead in a museum's glass case to understand the many networks within which an artifact can function. The arrowhead shares a relation with all the other objects in the case, often with the goal of providing an interpretation of a bygone way of life.

A useful way to view connectedness is through the concept of the Diderot unity. This term, now standard in the lexicon of consumer theory, allows us to grasp the significance of the relations experienced by all artifacts-as-commodities.

The Diderot Unity

Consumer anthropologist Grant McCracken developed the term the "Diderot unity" from an essay written by Denis Diderot in 1772. Diderot, today famed for his mid-eighteenth century *Encyclopédie* of French industry and commerce, wrote an intriguing essay pertinent to today's modern-world archaeology. One of the reasons why this short essay has gained such prominence outside academia, and why it has significance in modern-world archaeology, is that a number of activists for sustainable consumption have adopted it as a potent example of "affluenza," the condition of modern-day consumerism gone mad. Diderot's essay neatly linked present and past, one of the primary tasks of modern-world archaeology, even though Diderot wrote about a specific time and place as well as a unique personal circumstance. Once again we see the micro helping to conceptualize the macro.

In the essay Diderot pondered the ramifications of having received a new dressing gown as a gift from a friend. He used the essay to consider the impact of his new piece of finery on both his psyche and his physical surroundings. After thinking about it, Diderot discovered that he felt perfectly carefree while wearing the old dressing gown, but he felt oddly ill at ease in the new one. In the old gown, he neither worried about spilling tea on it nor was he shy about using its corner to wipe the dust from a book's cover. Blots of ink or sparks from the fireplace were no bother and a clumsy servant was of no concern. The stains and black streaks on the old gown were small badges of honor, tiny monuments to deep thought and hours devoted to the most profound philosophical introspections. In short, the old dressing gown was comfortable.

The new dressing gown changed all this. Wearing it Diderot felt that his image was that of a wealthy layabout, a parasitic member of the idle rich who was prone to devoting more time to his appearance than to the life of the mind. He now perceived his time spent pondering deep thoughts as less than honorable. He also discovered something else quite remarkable: that the presence of the new clothing also changes his immediate surroundings. The effects of the new gown were more than simply personal; they were also spatial. Diderot discovered that the new gown caused him to alter his material furnishings to conform to its newness. He began to understand that his new attire made everything around him appear shabby and worn. The new dressing gown was not simply a harmless piece of clothing designed to make him look better; it also destroyed the harmony of his study. To compensate he was driven to replace his old furniture. He replaced an old chair made of straw with one covered in Moroccan leather; bronze statues now stood in places once occupied by clay figurines and the old drapes disappeared. The simple dressing gown instilled elegance into Diderot's study and created a transformative process McCracken termed the "Diderot effect." The new gown's esteem-value caused Diderot's world to go askew.

The Diderot effect is what happens when a person attempts, like Diderot himself, to make his or her material surroundings consistent. Painting a room after buying new drapes or wearing nicer trousers after purchasing a new pair of shoes are examples. The effect is the act of making certain that a collection of artifacts exhibits conformity, with the assemblage being termed the "Diderot unity." In *Culture and Consumption: New Approaches to the Symbolic Character of Consumer Goods and Activities*, McCracken concisely summarized the significance of acknowledging the Diderot unity.

> It appears to be the case that consumer goods do not communicate well when they exist in isolation or in heterogeneous groups. The meaning of a good is best (and sometimes only) communicated when this good is surrounded by a complement of goods that carry the same significance. Within this complement, there is sufficient redundancy to allow the observer to identify the meaning of the good. In other words, the symbolic properties of material culture are such that things must mean together if they are to mean at all. (1990, p. 121)

McCracken thus argues that artifacts have a meaning that is communicated through their collectivity. The concept of the Diderot unity, however, has a broader implication because it suggests that all commodities should be evaluated through their collectivity rather than as individual examples of a more global process. This realization has significance for modern-world archaeology because of its overt commitment to investigating consumption, consumerism, and globalization in the post-1500 world. The fact that commodities—such as European trade goods intended for the native North American market—are typically sold to conform to other commodities reinforces the case.

The Diderot Unity in Modern-World Archaeology

Elsewhere I have suggested the potential utility of the concept of the Diderot unity but historical archaeologists have generally ignored it. I believe that this is an oversight. The psychology of acquisition is remarkably complex and many of its elements are not completely understood. Acquisition involves how we see ourselves and how we wish to be seen by others.

In his intriguing cultural history of shopping, entitled *I Want That! How We All Became Shoppers*, Thomas Hine presented nine passions that drive modern consumers into what he calls the "buyosphere." These passions—which help us imagine the important linkages that exist between consumption, created desire, and artifacts-as-commodities—are worth presenting in full (with minor variations).

- Power: the use of objects to assert authority and prove your worth.
- Responsibility: shopping as a nurturing activity.
- Discovery: going among strangers to trade and learn.
- Self-expression: the role of objects in a world where individuals' identities aren't fixed.
- Insecurity: the conspiracy of shoppers and sellers that conjures up the illusion of scarcity and creates fashion to enhance the eventfulness of life.
- Attention: the craving to have one's desires recognized but not judged.
- Belonging: the use of objects to forge communities of taste and rebel against mainstream thinking.
- Celebration: the ways in which shopping helps give meaning to various holidays.
- Convenience: the integration and entanglement of shopping with the rest of life.

Some of this may represent pop psychology but much of it is backed up by the latest research in neuroscience and evolutionary psychology. And though much of Hine's thinking relates strictly to the hyperconsumerism of today, we can also see several elements of his list that can be easily related to history. At the very least, his list indicates the complex nature of artifact acquisition—a subject perfectly in tune with the goals of modern-world archaeology.

Attempting to understand the collective meaning of entire artifact assemblages (as aggregates of objects that began their lives as commodities rather than as individual specimens) reveals important avenues of inquiry. For one thing the concept of the Diderot unity challenges modern-world archaeologists to question the role of the analogous artifact. For instance, does the presence of a copper kettle within a native North American society encourage the acquisition of iron knives and glass beads? Or is the Diderot unity merely a logical implication of mercantilism/capitalism because of the consumer's concern with acquisition? If the answer to the latter question is yes, then another interesting element of the post-1500 world presents itself.

I believe that further research will reveal the Diderot unity as in fact a feature of modernity, for the simple reason that only with mass consumption can we pick and choose what artifacts we wish to have around us. In non-capitalist societies, such as those encountered in pre-contact North and South America, people could only surround themselves with things directly from their local environments or with a few trade items (which were often luxury goods). Clay pots were consistent with stone projectile points, but were clay pots consistent with brass arrow points? Was consistency involved in the process of incorporating brass kettles into native contexts? Historical archaeologists have often tended to imagine that the transition from clay pots to brass kettles was simply an aspect of adaptation (or, earlier, of acculturation), but perhaps the transition is a working out of the Diderot unity.

An overriding question for modern-world archaeologists, as it is for consumer scientists, is "Why do people choose certain artifacts and not others?" We cannot answer this extremely complicated question here, but Pierre Bourdieu has provided one avenue of inquiry with the concept of taste.

TASTE

In *Distinction: A Social Critique of the Judgment of Taste*, sociologist Pierre Bourdieu rejected the rational actor model of consumption put forward by Adam Smith and others. The basis of his thinking derived from his concept of *habitus*. *Habitus* is an extremely complex concept and Bourdieu's own ideas about how to define it changed over time.

Put most simply, we can think of *habitus* as a set of beliefs, ideas, and expectations individuals adopt as part of their socialization process within the conditions of the social position of their class. The frameworks within which people operate are epochal structures, and the concept of *habitus* is compatible because it includes the power relations that help determine what is possible for individuals to achieve within the sociohistorical environment in which they live. The exercise of power is wholly relational, and most of Bourdieu's research focused on the ways in which social inequalities and privileges are sustained through generations in the absence of revolution. For Bourdieu, then, *habitus* mediates between economics (what an individual can afford; the measure of exchange-value) and commodity selection (what an individual desires; a measure of esteem- and/or use-value).

Bourdieu defined material preference as "taste." Taste is an expression of a person's position within networks of societal power, and the objects people select to surround themselves—the Diderot unity—exist in harmony with *habitus*. One important implication of this idea is that purchasing power alone does not always determine what commodities a person will choose because *habitus* works to maintain the consistency of the

Diderot unity. In other words, winning the lottery and becoming an instant multimillionaire does not push a garage mechanic into the top 1%, except perhaps economically. The mechanic's *habitus* will mediate her ideas about how to spend the windfall money and so culturally she will remain well within the 99%. To put this into Bourdieu's terms, her economic capital will be high but her cultural capital will be low. (If she is smart, however, she will use some of the money to send her children to an elite university, thus significantly increasing their stock of cultural capital.)

It is worthwhile to point out, however, that people cannot afford to purchase things that are beyond their means. Even if someone buys something on credit, failure to pay has significant legal consequences. As a result a connection exists between *habitus* and purchasing power, but the equation is still not entirely straightforward. Striking it rich in the lottery does not mean that the winner will suddenly acquire the taste of the elites. Money, viewed as existing outside *habitus*, does not equal taste. Elvis's Jungle Room at Graceland alone proves this fact.

The concept of commodity consistency, or the Diderot unity, helps us understand Bourdieu's "structures of consumption." His research in contemporary France demonstrated quite clearly that social classes purchase commodities that are consistent with the surrounding objects. One of his important findings was that a society's elite members practice "tastes of luxury" while nonelites practice "tastes of necessity." This distinction is significant because it highlights the material culture distance between "haves" and "have-nots" as it simultaneously brings to the fore the privilege inherent in having great amounts of economic capital. The introduction of the privilege residing within economic capital raises the specter of the struggles between social classes for the control of material culture, and Bourdieu saw social spaces as places of constant struggle. In their search for material distinction, elite members of society are easily able to convert their economic capital into cultural capital expressed by the rules of etiquette. Privileged elites can maneuver in a world where they can practice "consumer sovereignty," a position consistent with the concept of *habitus*.

Taste and Power

One of the key features of Bourdieu's views about taste that is particularly relevant to modern-world archaeology is the idea that each *habitus* embodies the material conditions in existence and that individuals with the most capital have the freedom to engage in the pursuit of "tastes of luxury," whereas individuals with considerably less capital are engaged in the pursuit of "tastes of necessity." It is precisely for this reason that elite members of the colonial Anglo world practiced the tea ceremony (see Chapter 1). The ideologies of mercantilism and especially capitalism—both of which are rooted in theories of individualism—maintain that elite taste derives from knowledge, desire, and access to wealth, rather than from pure necessity. The reality is that people having small amounts of economic capital must concern themselves with survival rather than the "finer things in life." The epochal structures of power within the sociohistorical moment in which they live establish these realities.

The inequalities of power represented in any social environment and expressed in material culture do not necessarily mean that all resistance is futile. Sustained resistance to an epochal structure is extremely difficult but people do struggle to create better lives for themselves. Modern-world archaeology is especially interested in documenting these struggles, and it is to this subject that we now turn—including other challenges faced by modern-world archaeologists.

SUGGESTED READINGS

Bourdieu, Pierre. 1984. *Distinction: A Social Critique of the Judgment of Taste.* Translated by Richard Nice. Harvard University Press, Cambridge, MA.

A complex but important study of the relationship between *habitus*, consumerism, and social position.

Diderot, Denis. 1956. *Rameau's Nephew and Other Works.* Translated by Jacques Barzun and Ralph H. Bowen. Doubleday, Garden City, NY.

Includes Diderot's famous musings about his new dressing gown. A fun read.

Hine, Thomas. 2003. *I Want That! How We All Became Shoppers.* Harper-Collins, New York.

A study of today's consumerism and how modern Westerners became such avid shoppers.

Hodder, Ian. 2011. Human-Thing Entanglement: Towards an Integrated Archaeological Perspective. *Journal of the Royal Anthropological Institute* 17:154–177.

An archaeologist's consideration of early twenty-first century views of the connections between humans and their things. Not modern-world archaeology, but worth reading.

McCracken, Grant. 1990. *Culture and Consumption: New Approaches to the Symbolic Character of Consumer Goods and Activities.* Indiana University Press, Bloomington, IN.

An important analysis of consumption from an anthropological point of view. Includes discussions of the Diderot unity and Diderot effect.

Olsen, Bjørnar. 2010. *In Defense of Things: Archaeology and the Ontology of Objects.* Altamira Press, Lanham, MD.
An up-to-date reevaluation of the role of artifacts in human life. Not modern-world archaeology, but a good consideration of some contemporary views.

STUDY QUESTIONS

1. What does it really mean to say that artifacts "mediate" between humans and other humans and between humans and their environments? Provide two examples of each.

2. Why are commodities so important to modern-world archaeology? Think about the ways archaeologists can study them in both local and global frames.

3. Think about the most recent commodity you have purchased. What social relationships did this process include? Did any social relationships develop because of the object you purchased?

4. Provide two concrete examples of artifacts in your own life that have esteem-value.

CHAPTER 7

CHALLENGES

Modern-world archaeologists will continually confront interpretive challenges because the world constantly changes. Not only does our own time move forward, but our understandings of the past change as we discover new things and rethink old ideas. We devise new ways to see history in an effort to discern fresh things within it. We hope that our interpretations reflect past reality as much as possible, but we are willing to concede our own fallibility. As the great French historian Marc Bloch once observed, the past itself cannot change, but we know that how we decide to envision it has meanings that shift and shudder along with time itself.

Modern-world archaeology strives to remain fresh and innovative at the same time that I hope it remains relatively free from the fads archaeologists often adopt as they seek answers to long-standing questions. Despite a willingness to stay current, modern-world archaeology must remain committed to the critical investigation of the "haunts" of modernity—colonialism, Eurocentrism, capitalism, and racialization. The mistaken charge that modern-world archaeology is inherently Eurocentric has been completely refuted and need not be addressed again. Studying the impacts, effects, and rejections of Europe's diverse plans and actions throughout the world since 1500 does not require an apology. That some neoconservative writers have revived the jingoistic mantra of national exceptionalism has nothing whatsoever to do with modern-world archaeology.

The refutation of a Eurocentric viewpoint does not mean that modern-world archaeology abandons the examination of Eurocentrism as a force in modern history (see Chapter 2). The tangible practices and outcomes of Eurocentrism have measurable consequences, and modern-world archaeologists acknowledge and appreciate the dialectics of inclusion and exclusion that have characterized metropolis-colony linkages since about 1500. Pre-1945-style colonialism may have receded into the past but it would be naive to imagine that core : periphery connections have disappeared. Only the names, places, and commodities have changed; the structures remain implacably stable. The rejection of Eurocentric attitudes, practices, and perspectives does not erase the significance of understanding the peripheries. Quite the contrary, modern-world archaeology demands a practical dialectics that necessarily situates indigenous peoples directly in the middle of all social situations that have occurred since about 1500.

THE MODERN WORLD

A central goal of modern-world archaeology is to investigate, interpret, and interrogate the world in which we live. It is a world that, as historian A. J. R. Russell-Wood observed in *The Portuguese Empire, 1415–1808: A World on the Move*, began with "contacts between Europeans and non-Europeans [that] inexorably heralded a new transcontinental, transoceanic, and transnational age of globalization which was to be characterized by interdependence, interaction, and exchange" (1992, p. xiv). This is the world within which we still struggle.

Modern-world archaeologists use the multidisciplinary tools of traditional historical archaeology to expand the boundaries of cultural knowledge, but modern-world archaeology does not embrace the shopworn platitude that "we study the past to understand the present." Modern-world archaeologists acknowledge that the present is more than a hazy reflection of the past. The past and the present constantly interact through our efforts of analysis and presentation. The precursor to our present was constructed by millions of individuals—myriad non-Europeans and Europeans alike—who created, maintained, and fought against the epochal structures in which they lived. We acknowledge at the same time that the dominant frameworks of the epochal structures were (and indeed are) designed, implemented, and enforced by each historical society's most powerful colonialists, capitalists, Eurocentrists, and racialists.

To state this, however, is not to accept its inevitability. History shows that indigenous peoples can often force the powerful to readjust or reevaluate elements of an epochal structure. Sometimes, as in the case of the successful slave rebellion in nineteenth century Haiti, their actions impel transformation. In far too many cases, though, ruptures in the epochal structures were intermittent or temporary, since those in power used their repressive authority to crush rebellion and stifle dissent. That revolts and resistances can even occur at all indicates that tensions and weaknesses exist within the epochal structures despite their apparent solidity.

Following the dictates of dialectical analysis, at least two classes must be jointly considered in any analysis that calls itself modern-world archaeology. If the modern history of racialization has included individuals who have been classified as "inferior," then by definition a group must exist that has deemed itself "superior." Slavery requires "enslavers" if an "enslaved" group exists, and capitalism needs both "laborers" and "owners" to operate. Simple dialectics means that opposites create the social whole and that the relations between them are often tense and fraught with danger. As a result colonial encounters were sociospatial places of conflict and cooperation, distance and proximity, and friendship and enmity.

Modern-world archaeology will continue to face a series of challenges as it struggles to attain relevance within general anthropological practice. Part of the ongoing challenge is to continue promoting the reality of the so-called "great divergence" that occurred as a result of the Columbian encounter. Some archaeologists—perhaps those not trained in traditional historical archaeology or not conversant with global history—continue to exclaim that history has no breaks. For them the uninterrupted flow of time means that life in 1000 was essentially similar to life in 1600. People are people and social relations are social relations. This view is appealing as a matter of common sense because we recognize it in the steady progression of our own lives. But who is willing to argue that our current smart-phone lives are identical to the time when we had to hunt for a working pay phone in a dark parking lot? Does anyone really believe that chronology does not matter and that human history has no disjunctions?

In this chapter I explore two topics that present challenges to modern-world archaeology. The first is represented by postcolonial theory, a paradigm initially proposed by writers and literary critics and slowly making its impact felt in contemporary archaeology. The second topic is the question of separation, or the social distance between archaeologists and their subjects.

POSTCOLONIALISM

Scholars writing from numerous disciplinary traditions have had difficulty defining "postcolonial" with clarity. An easy way to understand the term is by considering the difference between "post-colonial" and "postcolonial," a subtle but significant variation similar to that existing between world-systems and world systems (see Chapter 3). In common usage "postcolonial" (without the hyphen) refers to the general body of literature, theory, and perspective that helps frame an understanding of the cultural and historical impacts of the process of colonialism. This research is inherently based on unraveling the complex network of relations that were enacted between colonizers and colonized as a result of culture contact. On the other hand, "post-colonial" (with the hyphen) specifically refers to an era of political independence following the termination of a colonial regime. Thus we would write about the post-colonial history of India after 1947 but take a postcolonial approach to understanding twentieth century Indian history.

Because both terms refer to post-Columbian colonialism, the obvious question for modern-world archaeology is "Does the connection between postcolonialism and colonialism imply an overwhelming interest in only one of the haunts?" In other words, does the interest in postcolonialism push colonialism to the front of the queue, thereby prefiguring it as most important? One of the primary tenets of modern-world archaeology is that the haunts collaborate to create the modern world. So is colonialism the most important haunt?

In some ways the answer is "Yes." Eurocentrism, racialization, and capitalism would have far different characteristics in the absence of European expansion and colonialism. Eurocentrism and racialization may be possible on a nation-state level but capitalism without its global dreams is impossible to imagine. Even post-Columbian racialization was a product of European colonialism, and Europeanization (reshaped through time as Americanization) inherently encompasses global expansion. The union of the haunts as a transformative, worldwide force is what has given our world its current form. European expansion and colonialism are historical facts and historical archaeologists know it.

Defining Postcolonialism

Literary theorists have done much of the initial thinking and writing about postcolonialism but a good deal of their textual analyses has little direct application to archaeological research. Much of their work has excluded the historical and the material because they have chosen to concentrate on textual representations, their field of specialty. In adapting the major tenets of postcolonialism, modern-world archaeology seeks to contribute to understanding the materiality implied by postcolonial practice. As far as modern-world archaeology is concerned, the following description presented by Bill Ashcroft, Gareth Griffiths, and Helen Tifflin in *Key Concepts in Post-Colonial Studies* adequately outlined the pertinent aspects of postcolonial analysis.

> [T]he study and analysis of European territorial conquests, the various institutions of European colonialisms, the discursive operations of empire, the subtleties of subject construction in colonial discourse and the resistance of those subjects, and most importantly perhaps, the differing responses to such incursions and their contemporary colonial legacies in both pre- and post-independence nations and communities. While its use has tended to focus on the cultural production of such communities, it is becoming widely used in historical, political, sociological, and economic analyses, as these disciplines continue to engage with the impact of European imperialism upon world societies. (1998, p. 187)

In addition to colonialism, readers will observe the other haunts hiding within this quote. The idea of subject construction incorporates Eurocentrism and racialization, and the continuing engagement of non-European peoples with the long-lasting impacts of European imperialism raises the specter of capitalism and its most tenacious achievement—the globalization of mass consumerism. The postcolonialists' interest in pre- and post-independence states is entirely consistent with the present : past connections investigated in modern-world archaeology, especially since they took many of their first breaths with the advent of European global expansion after about 1500.

Four Elements of Postcolonial Analysis

At least four overarching elements of postcolonial analysis are also directly relevant to modern-world archaeology.

§ Because postcolonialism has an inescapable global dimension, its best analyses rely on interdisciplinary research. In failing to respect traditional academic borders, postcolonial researchers encourage dialogue between different intellectual traditions. Modern-world archaeologists—as historical archaeologists—would find it unwise, uninteresting, and nearly impossible to concentrate only on archaeological evidence and ignore all other lines of inquiry.

§ Like modern-world archaeology, postcolonial scholars do not expect or encourage univocality (the presentation of only one voice). Modern-world archaeologists do not agree with radical postmodernists who argue that there is no objective truth. Modern-world archaeologists do recognize that different perspectives can make it appear that disparate truths of a single historical narrative may exist, however. The use of multiscalar analysis in modern-world archaeology ensures that many truths might be revealed in any particular sociohistorical context and that these truths may appear to conflict. At the same time, however, modern-world archaeology accepts that the question of truth applies only to interpretations and not to empirical observations. The size and shape of a pit feature or a brick wall—and indeed their very existence—cannot be disputed empirically as "real."

§ Postcolonial researchers understand that the production of knowledge has political aspects that may or may not be intentional or even conscious. For modern-world archaeology this realization equates with the effort to make archaeological knowledge relevant—one of the major impetuses for thinking about modern-world archaeology in the first place. Without a socially constituted rationale, archaeology is in constant danger of being trivialized and denigrated as a mere hobby. Modern-world archaeology critiques the union of colonialism, Eurocentrism, capitalism, and racialization in post-Columbian history.

§ The use of postcolonial thought makes it impossible for historical archaeologists to ignore the cross-cultural encounters that characterize post-1500 global history. The concept of multicultural entanglements challenges us to think across time, to appreciate and understand modernity as complexly interconnected network structures that have been created in the post-Columbian past and present and within which all of us still struggle.

This last point conveys the belief in modern-world archaeology that the haunts impact the practice of contemporary archaeology. Their effect is especially strong in the historical archaeology of the post-Columbian world because the relevant networks extend vertically from the past to the present. To cite one example, the basic structure of nineteenth century racialization is still a force with which we must reckon today.

At its core postcolonial analysis represents a critique of colonialism, but it also includes all the elements studied in modern-world archaeology. Modern-world archaeology identifies the impacts of and struggles against colonialism, illuminates the power and influence of Eurocentric practices, uncovers the social reality of racialist categorizations, and explains the capitalist project. Its milieu of examination is post-1500 history.

The roots of postcolonial thought extend back at least to the comments of the sixteenth century Spaniard Father Bartolomé de las Casas, but a great many writers followed him in disparaging European nation-state conquests. Many of their comments contained material references. In the early nineteenth century, for example, Jeremy Bentham—an opponent of colonialism—equated happiness and security with material goods, which he referred to as the "class of things." Numerous late eighteenth and early nineteenth century philosophers regularly thought about the material elements of social life and many linked physical objects with the pursuit of happiness. The rise of mass consumerism that accompanied the growth of capitalism made this sort of thinking seem abundantly reasonable because the capitalist project was widely perceived as a force that would benefit all. A household full of things would make families more successful and happier.

Archaeologists have been relatively slow to adopt a postcolonial perspective. The reason for this reluctance is unclear. The cause may simply be that archaeologists tend to adopt new ideas only after they have been available for years in other disciplines; the so-called "theory lag" in archaeology is well known. As Jeremy Sabloff noted in *Archaeology Matters: Action Archaeology in the Modern World*, "[T]he field of archaeology has been a conservative one, and change does not come easily or rapidly to the discipline" (2008, p. 109). Accepting his position as true causes us to wonder why this is so.

New Ideas in Archaeology

In two important essays published in 1980 and 1984, renowned archaeologist Bruce Trigger offered his observations about archaeologists' hesitancy to adopt new perspectives. At the same time, he presaged the development of postcolonial archaeology.

Examining the era from the late 1790s to the 1930s, Trigger observed that archaeologists were extremely conservative throughout this time. In terms of North America pre-Columbian history specifically, intellectual conservatism meant that most archaeologists modeled American Indian cultures as static. They explained cultural change in terms of migration or diffusion because they believed internal change to be impossible. For them indigenous North Americans were not inventive enough to create new things on their own; they could only learn innovations from others. This approach, even when adopted unconsciously, denigrated indigenous cultures as it simultaneously promoted the view that only as a result of contact with Europeans could native peoples "advance." (Here we witness the combination of Eurocentrism and racialization evident in archaeological practice.)

Trigger's concern was solely with pre-European contact archaeology, but many of his comments equally apply to historical archaeology. Regarding the "classificatory-chronological" era, dating roughly from 1914 to 1960, Trigger stated that

> interpretations of archeological data were characterized by a lack of will to discover, or even to search for, any overall meaning to American prehistory. By contrast, European prehistory continued to be studied as a chronicle of the progressive development and achievements of the ancestors of particular European peoples, or of Europeans as a whole, even after a concern with ethnic groups had replaced evolutionary progress as the major focus of archaeological interest. (1980, p. 669)

Until recently historical archaeologists have generally failed to search for an overall meaning for their discipline beyond the platitude of "knowing the past to explain the present." Many practicing historical archaeologists may not have a well-developed personal understanding of why they practice archaeology. Some archaeologists, masters of artifact analysis, have substituted the nationalist cause of whole-culture reconstruction for a particularistic concern with artifact identification and dating. These concerns, albeit necessary for an informed archaeology to exist, cannot by themselves make historical archaeology into a socially relevant kind of anthropology.

Trigger observed that the development of ethnoarchaeology—the conduct of ethnographic fieldwork by archaeologists—had the promise to connect native peoples with archaeologists in new and important ways, but at the time he wrote relations between archaeologists and indigenous peoples were still strained. Many native peoples understood that even ethnoarchaeology, used insensitively or as an element of colonialist or imperialist archaeology, could be patronizing and exploitive rather than liberating and enlightening.

SEPARATION

Part of the problem inherent in the design of the archaeology Trigger wrote about stemmed from the separation it encouraged between archaeologists and non-archaeologists. Social distance often occurred because of the archaeologist's reliance on an overly bloated jargon, dense methodologies, labyrinthine statistical tests, and complicated computational algorithms hastily borrowed from the hard sciences. These ingredients served to mystify archaeology and set its practitioners apart as a select body of knowledgeable shamans who were allowed to possess the keys to understanding the past. Uninformed commoners—which would include non-Western peoples and undereducated Westerners alike—could not easily obtain entry into this world. In 2009 African archaeologist Ndukuyakhe Ndlovu provided a poignant personal account of the implications of this enforced separation, even for someone like him who was profoundly interested in archaeology as a career.

As Ndlovu documented, the separation of archaeological practice from the cause of living peoples had myriad practical implications in South Africa, where archaeology was often perfectly comfortable with apartheid. Many archaeologists in the country were accorded the benefits of their profession as long as they remained aloof from the politics of the present. This separation included the failure to discuss such controversial topics as indigenous rights and cultural property rights—precisely the subjects about which archaeologists ostensibly should know. As a result one curious paradox was that African archaeologists could study African history without ever thinking about actual living Africans as part of the vast historical sweep of human history. They saw the past/present gulf as something that did not concern them; living Africans were not part of history so they were not "archaeological."

Archaeologist Larry Zimmerman had earlier exposed a similar situation pertaining to the archaeology of Native Americans. He has written extensively about the social distance between archaeologists and the peoples whose histories they study, the mystification of archaeology through language and method, and the condescension with which many archaeologists have viewed descendant communities.

Archaeologists not having direct experience with the pre-1980s history of the discipline should understand the "self-delusion" of this era. Many archaeologists may not be aware of the hostility the archaeological profession in the United States expressed to the idea of American Indian cultural rights, including the right to rebury their dead ancestors and the right to cultural patrimony. Many might be surprised to learn, perhaps, that archaeologists who supported Indian rights (like Zimmerman) were labeled traitors to their profession, were denied academic positions and professional advancement, and had their manuscripts unfairly rejected for publication because they were "too political." This totalitarian strain within professional archaeology has significantly lessened today but it has not altogether disappeared. Much of the impetus for change came initially from outside the profession through the pressures exerted on archaeologists by indigenous activists. Some hardline archaeologists resented this "interference" and a few still view indigenous peoples suspiciously.

The development of postcolonial archaeology, when considered beside the haunts, raises the importance of separation to modern-world archaeology. My concept of separation arises from my original thoughts about the haunts and their relationships with contemporary archaeological practice (see Chapter 2). My views about this matter, first expressed in full in 1996, encapsulate one of the primary challenges facing the practice of modern-world archaeology: recognizing the role of the haunts in the cultural operation of the past and in the construction of the past in our present. This idea rests on the acknowledgment that an apolitical archaeology is impossible. Apathy, in both politics and scholarship, is still a political statement. Anyone who seriously continues to believe that archaeology does not have a political aspect should examine the heated controversies over the meaning of excavations in the West Bank.

ACKNOWLEDGING, UNDERSTANDING, AND CHALLENGING THE HAUNTS

One of the most important tasks of modern-world archaeology is to make historical archaeologists aware of what they are doing and why they are doing it. Such conscious self-reflection will only be achieved when archaeologists researching the past five centuries come to terms with the presence of colonialism, Eurocentrism, capitalism, and racialization within archaeological practice. The rise of postcolonial and collaborative archaeologies are helping to move this process forward, but traditional historical archaeology still has much to achieve in this regard. Historical archaeologists working as modern-world archaeologists must acknowledge, understand, and challenge the four haunts. Postcolonial archaeology demands precisely this in regard to colonialism, but modern-world archaeology maintains that it must also occur in relation to the other haunts as well.

Capitalism

No practicing archaeologist who is being honest should have to be told about the role that capitalism plays in contemporary archaeology. The heretofore-tacit links between archaeology and capitalism were laid bare with the development of commercial archaeology in the 1970s.

Historically, the archaeological profession was firmly in the hands of wealthy dilettantes or affluent middle-class professionals who had to rely on personal funds or the good graces of rich patrons to conduct their research. Despite differences in overall wealth, the capitalist class structure meant that these two groups had the leisure time, funds, education, and personal freedom to engage in what the laboring class undoubtedly perceived as a hobby that they could not pursue even by choice. In the United States, the GI Bill allowed some lower-middle-class individuals to attend college, but even this program left many talented individuals laboring in occupations completely alienated—to borrow a term from Marx—from subjects like archaeology.

This situation changed with the enactment of cultural preservation legislation in the 1970s. These laws, and those put in place in other nations, transformed archaeology into an attractive business opportunity. By 2005 a large percentage of professional archaeologists were employed in the corporate sector and were engaged in the study of threatened cultural resources. Surveys reveal that in 2005, 27.7% of professional archaeologists in the United States and 47.9% of professional archaeologists in Australia were commercially employed. As of this writing, most professional archaeologists worldwide are *not* employed by educational institutions.

Randall McGuire, writing in 2008, has ably recounted the way in which cultural resource management archaeology evolved with capitalism and how it reinforced the class system in the profession. His analysis showed that the wages of common field hands were low and artificially manipulated, the work was deskilled, and traditional archaeological education was deemphasized. Owners of cultural resource firms clearly understood capitalism well enough to appreciate the connection between wages and profits. In keeping with the general trend in higher education, at least in the United States, archaeological knowledge began to be based on technical aptitude rather than on critical thinking skills. Managers of commercial archaeology companies clamored for changes in the education of archaeology students so that workers could graduate with skills better suited to their corporate needs.

As new employees, graduates could be easily incorporated into the endless commercial treadmill that included survey and excavation, analysis, report writing, and proposal submission—followed by another round beginning with a new survey or excavation. University administrators who had adopted the business model of higher education eagerly urged their anthropology faculties to adapt to the new reality and many eagerly responded with courses suited to commercial research. McGuire refers to the laborers as the "archaeological proletariat," an entirely apt term because of their deep immersion in the capitalist project.

It would be unfair, however, to propose that only commercial archaeologists are engaged in the capitalist process. All archaeologists are enmeshed within it regardless of what they do in archaeology.

Understanding capitalism, as I have briefly discussed in Chapter 2, is an ongoing and difficult process. Many people, because they have been part of this system for so long, accept it as inevitable and natural. Politicians and the corporate media strive to reinforce the idea that capitalism is not just the best way to live, but that it is the only way. Archaeology will never change capitalism, but to challenge it archaeologists must first understand it. Here, then, we see the importance of Marx: love him or hate him, he truly understood the structural and historical subtleties of this system far better than most analysts.

Connections Between Present and Past

Archaeologists cannot single-handedly challenge capitalism or hope to transform it through the simple act of excavating a site. But archaeologists can use their knowledge to inform the public about circumstances and situations that have existed in the past and persist today. In an article published in 2011, I drew a direct link to the gap between the rich and the poor in the First Gilded Age (ca. 1875–1920) and the Second Gilded Age (ca. 1980–present). Both eras were characterized by phenomenal wealth and abysmal poverty. In describing the disparities in the First Gilded Age, I used works written in New York City and focused on neighborhoods that were geographically close to one another but worlds apart in terms of economic wealth. The terrible consistency of capitalism is well represented by Alex Gibney's 2012 film *Park Avenue: Money, Power, and the American Dream*, a documentary focusing on a single street in New York City connecting one of the most exclusive apartment buildings in the world on one end with the depths of American poverty and despair on the other. (This horizontal linkage also exhibits a vertical linkage through time, as shown by the comparison of the two American Gilded Ages.)

Many archaeologists have written about historical poverty, but in recent years some archaeologists have converted their interest in poverty into action by investigating homelessness. Larry Zimmerman's studies focus on homelessness in St. Paul, Minnesota, and Indianapolis, Indiana, while Rachael Kiddey and John Scholfield's study occurred in Bristol, England. Given the global nature of modern capitalism, no one should be surprised at the many similarities between the teams' findings—even though they conducted their studies thousands of miles apart. Both groups identified and documented sites that homeless individuals create and spoke directly with members of the homeless communities and their advocates.

What is most encouraging about these studies for the future of archaeology, however, is that both the American and British teams perceive their work as activism—meaning that both envision their archaeological efforts in terms of modern problems and living peoples. Even more encouraging is that the findings of both teams attracted widespread interest far beyond the narrow boundaries of archaeological research. Civic leaders, law enforcement officials, and community organizers consulted the archaeologists to discover what they had learned and to assess whether this knowledge could help them address the needs of the homeless.

The research conducted by these committed archaeologists is consistent with the overall goals of modern-world archaeology because it visibly demonstrates the importance of archaeological research to contemporary society. Homelessness itself dates to dynastic Egypt, but the goal of modern-world archaeology is to study it within capitalist practice in order to denaturalize it—to demonstrate that homelessness is not merely a feature of human existence but that its presence, toleration, and continuation supports global capitalism both in the past and the present. Only by acknowledging its power, understanding its structure and nuances, and challenging its naturalized existence can archaeologists become activists in ways they might not otherwise have thought possible.

Eurocentrism

The connections between archaeological practice and Eurocentrism are not as obvious today as they have been in the past. The rise of postcolonial thinking and other critical approaches to knowledge have ensured that Eurocentrism has been largely excised from archaeological practice. Feminist archaeologists have done a superb job of exposing the androcentric features of Eurocentrism, and others have demonstrated how writers of archaeological atlases and other compendia have tended to foreground ancient European and North American history while overlooking the cultural histories of Asia, Africa, and South America.

Inquiries of this nature significantly move the discipline of archaeology toward a much less Eurocentric practice and help foster a more global appreciation of human history. Nonetheless, it remains entirely possible for archaeologists to be tacitly Eurocentric in their failure to interrogate some of the taken-for-granted propositions in post-Columbian history. In accepting some features of history as inevitable or in not questioning their origins, archaeologists run the risk of perpetuating some of the wrongs of the past. Modern-world archaeology understands that Eurocentrism, though pernicious, is always possible if archaeologists do not engage in self-examination and critique.

Eurocentrism in Scholarship

In his critical investigation entitled *Eight Eurocentric Historians*, J. M. Blaut presented "Thirty Reasons Why Europeans Are Better Than Everyone Else (A Checklist)." He identified these thirty reasons within the works of the eight historians whose works he analyzes. All thirty are important for historical archaeologists to acknowledge, but #12 (that "Europeans were uniquely inventive") is perhaps most immediately relevant because it relates specifically to material culture. Blaut noticed that in promoting the cause of European exceptionalism, seven of the historians whose works he examined employed technological determinism as one explanation for Europe's "advantage" over Asia and Africa. The general idea is that Europeans, because of their innate inventiveness, have simply designed more efficient tools than other peoples. These technological marvels allowed them to become masters of the seas and lords of the land.

The development of the Portuguese caravel stands out as one of the most oft-cited examples of the inventiveness of rationalist Europeans. This hearty little ship of sixty tons, with its stern rudder and choice of square or triangular sails, allowed Portuguese sailors to explore the African coast at least fifty years before Columbus reached the Caribbean. After packing the holds full of desirable trade goods, captains could sail these vessels up rivers and into estuaries, reaching native villages eager to obtain new possessions. In this telling the Portuguese were able to establish a long-lasting mercantile presence outside Europe because their ships were simply superior to those of other nation-states. The caravel laid the groundwork for the rise of Portugal as a global superpower, despite the country's small size and tiny population.

This impressive narrative speaks convincingly to the inventiveness of Portuguese marine engineers until we recognize that the idea for the caravel originated in the Arab dhow. Without this non-European model, the Portuguese may have taken their voyages later—or perhaps not at all.

The example of the caravel's origin shows that the remnants of Eurocentrism might be found in contemporary historical archaeology—not in the overt belief of European greatness, but rather in overlooking (or perhaps merely not seeing) the contributions of non-Europeans to the so-called "European story." This is a subtle but important issue that modern-world archaeology seeks to resolve through its open dedication to multiscalar, global analysis. A class of object well known to historical archaeologists, tin-glazed earthenware, offers a useful lesson.

The Myth of European Tin-Glazed Earthenware

The manufacture of tin-glazed earthenware in Europe (faience, majolica, and delft) has deep multicultural roots, even though its association with European potters is irrefutable. But archaeologists who overlook the multicultural network connections buried within the history of tin-glazed earthenware might easily be considered to be guilty of muted Eurocentrism. Rather than being perfectly "European," the production of tin-glazed earthenware—even in the finest pothouses on the continent—links various Asian, European, and Middle Eastern polities in complex, historically sensitive ways.

Ceramic historians believe that Persian potters invented the process of glazing ceramic vessels with tin sometime in the ninth century. Moorish potters are thought to have introduced the method into the Iberian Peninsula and from there it traveled to Italy. Its history, however, is intimately linked to Chinese porcelain.

Well before the thirteenth century, Chinese merchants had participated in an international trade in porcelain, with their major trading partners living in India and the Middle East. For decades Islamic traders had marveled at the quality of the Chinese porcelain they encountered during their travels, and well before the mid-sixteenth century the principal non-Chinese consumers of porcelain lived in the Islamic world. So important was the Chinese : Middle Eastern connection that ceramists believe that the blue-and-white porcelain industry may not have developed as it did without Muslim interest.

As early as the Yuan dynasty (1279–1368), Islamic patrons had been able to impose their decorative aesthetics on Chinese potters, who were only too eager to decorate their export wares with verses from the Quran and other images that would appeal to their elite Muslim customers. Chinese potters adopted underglaze painting, an Islamic technique probably first used in Damascus in the twelfth century. To further ensure the appeal of their wares, Chinese potters also imported the rich cobalt oxide pigment called "Mohammedan blue" from the Middle East. At the same time, a number of Islamic potters began producing their own imitations of Chinese vessels.

Portugal had established direct contact with Beijing between 1517 and 1521, and its merchants successfully created the mechanics of the east-west trade in porcelain as a result. In response to the huge demand for porcelain in Europe, the Ming emperor decided to transform the city of Jingdezhen from a small market town into a major porcelain-producing industrial center. His goal was to mass-produce a saleable commodity purely for export and European consumers were only too eager to obtain it. In fact, Chinese merchants discovered that Europeans would accept pieces that the Chinese themselves viewed as inferior. A ewer produced in China around 1520, but made in an Islamic shape, provides a fitting example because the Portuguese coat of arms is painted upside down. We see in this one vessel the presence of Chinese, Middle Eastern, and Iberian connections.

Muslims living in the Arabian Peninsula and further inland in Persia also desired Asian porcelains, and here again clear links between Asia and the Middle East are expressed in material culture. A tin-glazed floor tile made in Antwerp, dating to sometime after 1570 and excavated in London, provides another visual clue to a non-European linkage by its representation of a camel—an animal forever associated with the exoticism of the Middle East.

Multicultural Porcelain

Once it became widely known, all European nations sought the exotic foreign porcelains, and the first large shipment of blue and white vessels to enter the Dutch United Provinces came by way of a captured Portuguese ship in 1602. For their part the Spanish sent vast amounts of silver (forcibly extracted from Peruvian mines as an element of colonialism) to Asia in exchange for porcelains. Chinese potters, willing to peddle what they considered to be inferior goods, sold porcelain vessels by the hundreds of thousands to willing Europeans. Between 1602 and 1650, Europeans imported millions of dishes, with most of them going into the Dutch trade or at least being funneled through Dutch merchants. Shipwrecks provide irrefutable proof of the enormous number of porcelain vessels exported from Asia during the colonial era.

Shortly after realizing that Chinese porcelain could stimulate consumer demand, potters in Spain, Portugal, and Mexico decided to imitate it with the technology they had, which was tin-glazed earthenware. These Ibero-American potters painted their vessels with designs they presumed were copies of Chinese motifs, but they often missed the mark by a wide margin. The same may be said for potters in the Ottoman Empire who attempted to imitate "the Oriental." Since they had no direct experience with China or the Chinese, the potters' decorations could be bizarre caricatures of Chinese motifs.

One of the most popular decorations among the Dutch was the Wan-li pattern, characterized by a broad border painted with large blue chrysanthemums on a bluish-white background. These faux-Chinese patterns were so popular that Dutch painters often included them in their still life studies. For example, Hubert van Ravensteyn's *Still Life of a Flower, Glass, Stoneware Jug, and Walnuts in a Chinese Bowl on a Ledge*, painted around 1670, depicts a beautiful Wan-li bowl holding walnuts. The appearance of tin-glazed Chinese copies in works of art was a continuation of the earlier depictions of fine Chinese porcelain by European painters working for wealthy patrons during the Renaissance.

Once trade became formalized in the early seventeenth century, English delftware potters adopted vessel forms and decorations used by Chinese and Japanese potters. Blue and white bowls, mugs, vases, and other forms became much-desired consumer goods for about two hundred years. They were standard pieces throughout Europe but were particularly associated with Great Britain and the Netherlands during the seventeenth and eighteenth centuries.

Even this brief exploration proves that to comprehend the true character of the tin-glazed "European" industry, we must think in multicultural terms. Its links to Asian porcelain are clear, although in the case of Chinese Export Porcelain historical archaeologists might initially think only in terms of a relatively straightforward Asian : European connection. Even the term implies this connection. But the term is a misnomer when viewed as a multiscalar artifact because the network that existed was more accurately a Chinese : Japanese : European network. Japanese traders imported their own porcelain into China at the same time that pieces of Dutch delft were finding their way into Japan. Even the use of "European" in this equation is inaccurate because the network connections expressed by tin-glazed earthenware linked together (at a minimum) England, the Netherlands, France, Italy, Portugal, Spain, and other nations. During the sixteenth century, when tin-glazed wares were still relatively novel, many European kings encouraged the best foreign potters to leave their homes and set up shop in their kingdoms. The royals' goal was to acquire the scarce luxuries before enterprising potters could begin to mass-produce and commoditize them at home.

Ceramics and Networks

The blue and white faience and delftwares that historical archaeologists identify at early colonial sites and associate with European potters thus have their roots in the network connections that existed much earlier between non-European and Asian traders. Dutch traders first encountered Chinese porcelain in the 1590s on the Indian subcontinent, and the Portuguese—who conquered Goa in the early sixteenth century—had learned about porcelain through this colonial experience. The distinctive "Europeaness" of blue and white faience and delft, therefore, can be questioned, but only once historical archaeologists acknowledge and understand its cross-cultural history.

The danger for historical archaeologists not practicing modern-world archaeology is that they may fail to appreciate the long evolution of blue and white tin-glazed earthenwares and their close associations with the Islamic world through the history of Middle Eastern : Asian connections. This failure—in and of itself—will not damage the profession, but it does contain a vestige of Eurocentrism because it silences the importance of the Islamic connection in European history. Modern-world archaeology challenges historical archaeologists to remember the large-scale, intercultural connections when they investigate history. Only once we acknowledge and understand that the failure to document interculturality represents a tacit Eurocentrism can we challenge its presence in historical archaeology. Silencing the roles and significance of Middle Eastern, African, Indian, and Asian interconnections in European colonialist and capitalist history will limit our abilities to challenge Eurocentrism in all its persistent forms. A single piece of blue and white delft can help us remember the world at large.

Racialization

The recognition of racialization has only occurred within historical archaeology since about 2000. As noted in Chapter 2, racialization is a deceitful process because its character changes through time, even though its basic structure of creating "us" and "them" remains remarkably intact.

One of the challenges confronting modern-world archaeology is to continue making the case that the process of racialization does not affect people of color alone. With the incredible explosion of African-American ar-chaeology in the United States and the Caribbean, the danger exists that ar-chaeologists will fail adequately to appreciate that racialization affects everyone, not just those people who have been racialized as inferior because of skin color. Personal physical characteristics are by far the most visible features that cause people to be racialized and their significance in this pernicious process must never be overlooked. But one of the goals of modern-world archaeology is to make the case that racializers can also tar-get culture, language, dress, religion, and lack of wealth as much as phys-ical appearance. The development of white studies certainly helps define the racialization process as related to more than dark skin color, but his-torical archaeologists must acknowledge the relevance of cultural features before a full appreciation of the racialization process can be developed. Racialization is quite literally not just a black-and-white issue.

In my two books on the importance of recognizing race and racializa-tion in historical archaeology, I consciously decided against focusing on people of African heritage—even though issues involving Africans in the New World are never far from the surface, if not explicitly mentioned. My plan was to impress upon historical archaeologists that the racialization process encompasses more than just Africans, and to accomplish this I highlighted the Irish (in Ireland and the United States) and Chinese immi-grants in the United States. In Ireland the English racialized the Gaelic Irish as an inferior Other because of their lifestyle, religion, and language—even though they shared many of the same physical characteristics as the Eng-lish. As pastoralists who spoke a Goidelic language and practiced Roman Catholicism, they were unlike their English overlords who were Anglican, spoke a Germanic language, and had agricultural roots. In the United States, these same Irish men and women suffered because of their religion and culture in a not-so-subtle continuation of their experiences in Ireland. Anglo-Saxon nativists feared the immigrants' Catholicism and, in the post-famine era (after circa 1850), hated them for their poverty. The Chinese also had religious and cultural attributes that set them apart from Anglo-Saxon America, but they had the added racial burden of looking different. Their clothing, names, and hairstyles also contributed to their Otherness.

The racialization of Irish and Chinese peoples demonstrates that racial-ization can be based on physical appearance but can also be attached to dress, language, and other cultural characteristics. We must also under-stand, however, that people can be racialized for noncultural reasons as well. One of the most malignant forms of persistent racialization involves poverty.

The racialization of the poor because of their lack of wealth is buried within the capitalist class structure. The process of racializing the poor is so tightly encapsulated within capitalism that it can be difficult to discern, especially by archaeologists examining assemblages of material culture. But the secret union of racialization and capitalism merely serves to demonstrate how the haunts are entangled in the modern world and how difficult it is to disentangle them except heuristically.

Working-Class Racialization

One subject that has received far too little attention in historical archaeology is the racialization of the working class. Some archaeologists have begun to address this subject, but most normally approach it as a class issue rather than as the combination of class and racial assignment. The distinction between class and racial assignment is complex and subtle, but at the most basic level class has an economic basis while racialization is an ideological layer applied to class distinctions. No inherent reason exists to explain why class standing by itself should involve discrimination, if not for the ideological component of capitalism that posits that those with greater financial resources have more societal consequence than those with less. In this telling the well-to-do are simply "better" than everyone with less economic capital.

In *London Labour and the London Poor*, Henry Mayhew used contemporary ethnological understandings to posit the existence of "two distinct and broadly marked races, viz. the wanderers and the settlers—the vagabond and the citizen—the nomadic and the civilised tribes." These two "races" constituted identifiable collectivities of individuals who, Mayhew believed, were distinctly visible within "civilized" society. In addition to these two extremes, the ethnographers whom he consulted also identified people who both wandered and settled. Expanding on this idea in the context of nineteenth century England, Mayhew identified the "habitual vagrant" and the "mechanic on tramp" as the polar extremes and "pedlars, showmen, harvest-men, and all that large class who live by either selling, showing, or doing something through the country" as the "mediate varieties." He also included urban and suburban wanderers, individuals who plied various trades in cities to gain enough money to survive (1861, Vol. I, p. 371).

But while focusing primarily on the wanderers' modes of subsistence, Mayhew also saw fit to racialize them by attaching physical characteristics to them. He was unable to explain the proximate cause of their physical difference, but concluded that they were more animal than human in terms of intellect and morality and that they could be distinguished physically (their high cheekbones and protruding jaws), linguistically (their use of slang rather than "proper" English), and materially (for their loosely defined concepts of private property). He further observed that they hated hard labor, rejected the idea of feminine honor, loved cruelty, and lacked religious belief. Mayhew thus succinctly included all the elements that can be used to racialize identifiable groups of people besides physical appearance—morality, language, religiosity, and temperament. The tenacity of racializating the nomad within capitalism can be observed today in the so-called "New Europe," where immigrants from developing nations are often pejoratively categorized as "new savages."

Some readers might conclude that this passage merely exposes Mayhew's own personal prejudices, and this is undoubtedly true. At the same time, however, the ideas he expressed were commonly held by elite members of English society. And tribalizing the poor was not restricted to Britain: the global structure of capitalist distinction made its presence felt in the United States, too. For example, writing of his visit to the Five Points in New York City in 1834, American hero Davy Crockett opined that he would risk an Indian fight rather than go into the area after dark. Why? Because he thought that the people who lived there were "worse than savages." (Crockett thus demeans two peoples at once: unassimilated Native Americans and the immigrant—mostly Irish—urban poor.)

Such distinctions were not always made because of physical appearance. The children of the late nineteenth century English working poor often felt oppressive hatred because of their clothes and hair, and the continuation of this imposed sense of shame through time and place demonstrates the structural realities of racialization in capitalist settings. Various studies of women receiving public assistance in the United States in the 1990s have revealed that many women have felt totally dominated by the process and in a state of complete submission to the powers-that-be. These examples represent the power of racialization to impact peoples based on characteristics having little to do with skin color or other physiological attributes.

Poverty and Racialization

Official records cannot expose the true horrors of poverty, especially for working families who cannot make financial ends meet but who do not appear in poverty statistics. For this information we must turn to first-hand narratives by the working poor, carefully researched microhistories, and sensitive accounts of daily life compiled by observant, honest scribes. A number of such accounts exist but an especially intriguing example appears in George Orwell's *The Road to Wigan Pier.*

Today, of course, Orwell is widely known and either admired or hated for *Animal Farm* and *Nineteen Eighty-Four.* But in addition to these works of socialist fiction, he also wrote first-hand social anthropology texts in which he recounted his experiences among the English working classes. He researched and wrote *The Road to Wigan Pier* for the Left Book Club, a socialist group that was interested to learn the realities of working-class life in England's industrial north. To write the book, Orwell traveled northwest from London and lived with coal miners and others who were either working in demeaning, difficult jobs or looking for work. Without question Orwell had his own well-known prejudices and biases, but his vision of working life in this one part of England in the 1930s is perceptive.

One of the most interesting features of Orwell's account is his discussion of the racialized differences he perceived within England itself. He notes, for instance, that

> when you go to the Industrial North you are conscious, quite apart from the unfamiliar scenery, of entering a strange country. This is partly because of certain real differences which do exist, but still more because of the North-South antithesis which has been rubbed into us for such a long time past. There exists in England a curious cult of Northernness, a sort of Northern snobbishness. A Yorkshireman in the South will always take care to let you know that he regards you as an inferior. . . . Hence the Southerner goes north, at any rate for the first time, with the vague *inferiority-complex of a civilized man* venturing among *savages*, while the Yorkshireman, like the Scotchman, comes to London in the spirit of a *barbarian* out for loot. (1937, pp. 109–110; emphasis added)

The truth of such observations might be questioned, but what is especially engrossing is the linkage between inferiority and place within a single nation-state and the association of place with physical characteristics. In analyzing these distinctions, Orwell observed that "[a]ll nationalistic distinctions—all claims to be better than somebody else because you have a different-shaped skull or speak a different dialect—are entirely spurious, but *they are important so long as people believe in them*" (1937, p. 111; emphasis added). This statement neatly demonstrates the ideological component of the capitalist class structure and exposes how racialization binds itself to it, becoming the rationale for the identification of difference.

Identifying the racialization process is difficult because it hides so neatly within the other haunts. It can be found within colonialism, capitalism, and Eurocentrism, where it resides quite comfortably. But its disguise is precisely the point. Its ability to hide makes it especially difficult to discern in archaeological assemblages and practice. Archaeologists must acknowledge and understand its presence among all peoples, not just those who have dark skin. Only once historical archaeologists fully accept what this means to them and their analyses will they finally be able to challenge the racialization process in the modern world in substantive ways.

CONCLUSION

The few challenges I have mentioned in this chapter suggest just a part of the difficulty historical archaeologists will face when attempting to practice modern-world archaeology. Many archaeologists may be willing to acknowledge and understand the presence of the four haunts both in the past and in their own research. Others, however, may be considerably less willing either to acknowledge or understand them, believing that their analysis does not fall within the purview of archaeological practice.

The greatest hesitancy will probably involve capitalism because of two major factors: the prevalence of commercial archaeology as a necessary livelihood for those outside the academy, and the existing class system within the academy. Archaeologists relying on cultural resource management incomes may be unwilling to interrogate capitalist practice for a purely practical reason: their corporate sponsors probably would not welcome projects with this agenda. Federal legislation concerning the protection of historical and cultural entities is usually rooted in the ideology of an "unimpassioned, objective" archaeology rather than the critiques modern-world archaeologists may offer. Many well-situated professors may not wish to scrutinize elements of the haunts that may impact their universities or colleges.

Without question the most difficult test facing modern-world archaeology involves challenging the haunts. This aspect of modern-world archaeology will undoubtedly take several years to be realized, but the signs of progress outside modern-world archaeology are encouraging. Many archaeologists are now working directly with indigenous and descendant communities and are recognizing that their research belongs to the present. Many archaeologists are learning from their collaborators and are willing to listen to non-Western forms of knowledge. Increasing numbers of archaeologists are accepting that history and culture, past and present, are profoundly entwined both vertically and horizontally.

Modern-world archaeology will not be easy to practice. On the contrary, I fully accept the difficulty in attempting to appreciate the interconnections between the haunts and the many transformations of their expressions over time and space. The archaeologist's necessary concentration on one discrete, relatively small place at a time makes modern-world archaeology inherently challenging. The archaeologist's gaze is understandably directed toward understanding how the people in a household, neighborhood, or village lived and looking beyond this small area is often extremely difficult. The true challenge of modern-world archaeology is to develop a dialectical vision that permits imagining the many frames—the many worlds—in which real individuals in the past lived.

SUGGESTED READINGS

Ashcroft, Bill, Gareth Griffiths, and Helen Tiffin. 1998. *Key Concepts in Post-Colonial Studies*. Routledge, London.
An extremely useful overview of postcolonial thinking.

Blaut, J. M. 2000. *Eight Eurocentric Historians*. Guilford Press, New York.
A classic examination of how eight famous historians used Eurocentrism without self-reflection.

Chibber, Vivek. 2013. *Postcolonial Theory and the Specter of Capital*. Verso, London.
This is a serious consideration of postcolonial theory. Perhaps difficult for the student just coming to postcolonial theory, but a required source.

Kiddey, Rachael, and John Schofield. 2011. Embrace the Margins: Adventures in Archaeology and Homelessness. *Public Archaeology* 10:4–22.
An archaeological study of homelessness in Bristol, England. Helps demonstrate how historical archaeology is maturing as a serious discipline.

Liebmann, Matthew, and Uzma Z. Rizvi (editors). 2008. *Archaeology and the Postcolonial Critique*. AltaMira Press, Lanham, MD.
A number of authors discuss the ways in which a postcolonial perspective is changing the ways archaeologists think about and interpret colonial encounters throughout the world.

Lydon, Jane, and Uzma Z. Rizvi (editors). 2010. *Handbook of Postcolonial Archaeology*. Left Coast Press, Walnut Creek, CA.
Presents a number of international overviews of the state of postcolonial archaeology.

McGuire, Randall H. 2008. *Archaeology as Political Action*. University of California Press, Berkeley.
A Marxist perspective on the role of archaeology in today's world. Well worth reading.

Ndlovu, Ndukuyakhe. 2009. Decolonizing the Mind-Set: South African Archaeology in a Postcolonial, Post-Apartheid Era. In *Postcolonial Archaeologies in Africa*, edited by Peter R. Schmidt, pp. 177–192. School for Advanced Research Press, Santa Fe, NM.
An important personal statement about archaeological activities in southern Africa. Demonstrates many of the political aspects of contemporary archaeological practice.

Orser, Charles E., Jr. 2011. The Archaeology of Poverty and the Poverty of Archaeology. *International Journal of Historical Archaeology* 15:533–543.
This article presents my comparison of the two Gilded Ages in American history.

Sabloff, Jeremy A. 2008. *Archaeology Matters: Action Archaeology in the Modern World*. Left Coast Press, Walnut Creek, CA.

Provides significant statements about the role of archaeology in today's world by a prominent and well-respected archaeologist. Must reading.

Trigger, Bruce G. 1980. Archaeology and the Image of the American Indian. *American Antiquity* 45:662–676.

Trigger, Bruce G. 1984. Alternative Archaeologies: Nationalist, Colonialist, Imperialist. *Man* 19:355–370.

Two articles in which the author, an internationally respected archaeologist, considers the practice of archaeology up to the 1980s. Provided much of the impetus for the development of postcolonial and other archaeologies, including modern-world archaeology.

Zimmerman, Larry J. 1992. Archaeology, Reburial, and the Tactics of a Discipline's Self-Delusion. *American Indian Culture and Research Journal* 16:37–56.

An important early statement by a prominent archaeologist about the social distance between archaeologists and indigenous peoples that once characterized archaeology. At the leading edge of archaeological thinking at a time when its ideas were not universally accepted.

Zimmerman, Larry J., and Jessica Welch. 2011. Displaced and Barely Visible: Archaeology and the Material Culture of Homelessness. *Historical Archaeology* 45:67–85.

An archaeological consideration of homelessness in St. Paul, Minnesota, and Indianapolis, Indiana.

STUDY QUESTIONS

1. Identify and discuss two features of postcolonial archaeology and explain why you think they are so important in helping us to understand the modern world.

2. Explain the concept of "separation" as used in this chapter.

3. Provide some reasons why you think so many archaeologists were opposed to working with American Indians until very recently. Do you think archaeological practice was helped or harmed by the general reluctance of archaeologists to engage with non-archaeologists, especially native peoples?

4. Explain two reasons why you think historical archaeologists, until very recently, overlooked the multicultural characteristics of modern-world artifacts. Why are things different now?

CHAPTER 8

THE FUTURE OF MODERN-WORLD ARCHAEOLOGY

As I have indicated throughout this book, it is unlikely that every historical archaeologist will decide to practice modern-world archaeology. I know from personal experience gained over the past several years that historical archaeology, in the United States at least, tends to be a conservative field. Until quite recently most historical archaeologists have avoided controversial issues, preferring to immerse themselves in the particularism of one site or region of interest and ignore broader questions. The rise of postcolonial archaeology and recent discussion about an anarchist perspective offer positive signs of hope.

Change may be in the air, but it is worth remembering that the roots of historical archaeology rest within a nationalist ideology and the urge to use historical archaeology for nationalist purposes can always return. The often-overt nationalism of the past allowed only certain sites to be preserved and presented to the public. Many archaeologists would not wish to surrender their expertise in promoting the historical and cultural uniqueness of the United States, nor would everyone be politically comfortable doing so. Historically, grant monies have been much easier to obtain if archaeology stays focused myopically on the past.

One dramatic change in recent historical archaeology concerns the study of the cultural histories of people of African descent. In fact, this area of research has exploded to the point that the subject now has its own journal and newsletter, and a cadre of dedicated scholars is diligently pursuing histories once kept hidden. But this is a recent occurrence. The careful student of the history of historical archaeology can easily locate reports of plantation excavations that do not even mention the enslaved. In such cases the archaeologist's sole attention was directed toward the lives of the wealthy and famous who inhabited the mansions. Will historical archaeology return to this line of investigation?

I doubt that archaeologists will overlook slavery ever again, and my hope is that young scholars adopt modern-world archaeology because I believe it offers a strong alternative to nationalist (and culturalist) archaeology. All historical archaeologists should be well versed in the history of their discipline, but this does not mean that anyone must be encumbered by its past shortcomings. The dedication being shown by practitioners working with indigenous and descendant communities or investigating poverty is a positive indication that historical archaeology's overall direction might be changing, but only time will tell. Sometimes the best ideas only receive attention until the next intellectual fad comes along.

One of the reasons I believe so strongly in modern-world archaeology, and why I continue to write about it even though its impact seems small at present, is rooted in my belief that the archaeology of the past five centuries is far more relevant than other archaeologies. I realize that this statement is controversial because it privileges one pursuit over another. Such a judgment appears prejudicial and unfair, so further explanation is required. The key to understanding my position stems from my view of relevance and its centrality within modern-world archaeology.

WHY IS RELEVANCE SO CENTRAL?

I have often made reference, here and elsewhere, to the need for archaeology to be relevant. A number of archaeologists have addressed and continue to address relevance through their collaboration with cultural elders, community leaders, and local historians, and this is all to the good. When I write about relevance, however, I refer specifically to the broad social relevance of the archaeology of the past five hundred years rather than to archaeology in general. I readily accept the "knowledge-for-knowledge's sake" argument and agree that all archaeological research has inherent merit. But my position is that this view is inadequate for explaining the relevance of modern-world archaeology. In other words, I believe that the archaeology of the past five centuries is too important to be clustered with the archaeologies of all other historical periods simply because it adds to our storehouse of knowledge about the human condition.

I take it as given that archaeology has made many extremely interesting and important discoveries over the past one hundred years and that these finds have significantly enriched our understanding of human history. In no way do I wish to denigrate the importance of archaeological research. Museum visitors, students taking archaeology courses, young children fascinated by pyramids, and heritage tourists have had abundant hours of enjoyment when encountering aspects of the human past—both tangible and intangible. Increased, widespread knowledge about the commonalities we share today with all those peoples who have gone before us can make a lasting contribution toward creating a just world. For many people the beauty and antiquity of artifacts is enough to give them an appreciation of history. Again, this is all to the good; the dissemination of archaeological knowledge to the public advances the profession of archaeology, just as it provides for the creation of educational materials and promotes a cross-cultural appreciation for art, architecture, and culture.

Most people (including most professional archaeologists) are fascinated by ancient things and faraway places. The very presence of the ancient evokes mystery and intrigue. But the attitude that "old is better" has undoubtedly been an impediment to the development of the historical archaeology of the past five centuries. A once-prevalent view, even in my archaeological lifetime, was that the most recent centuries were decidedly not the purview of archaeologists. Archaeologists who entered the profession after historical archaeology became a more respected pursuit may not imagine how negatively some archaeologists once reacted to the study of the most recent centuries. Not too long ago, many conference organizers would not accept papers or sessions dealing with post-Columbian topics and historical archaeologists had difficulty obtaining academic positions in anthropology departments that did not "do history." The reaction was similar to that described in Chapter 7 regarding those archaeologists who had the foresight to collaborate with native peoples. Thankfully, the tireless work of many professionals has changed the negative perception of historical archaeology, and today instructors in higher education teach the subject throughout the world.

The reasons for the often-angry reception of historical archaeology by non-historical archaeologists are unclear. To my knowledge the objectors have not explained their positions in writing. But as a practitioner of the archaeology of the recent past exclusively (I have never excavated at a pre-Columbian site; thus I did not fall into historical archaeology by default but rather adopted it as a career from the beginning), I have often wondered whether the "problem" with the archaeology of the most recent centuries is simply because of its relevance to our own times. Strictly speaking, the issue is not that its subject is not old enough, but that it is too new.

Is the Modern World Too Recent?

This realization was in my mind for several years but I really began to appreciate its possibility as an explanation when I began working in Ireland. My goal was to work specifically in the era of the Great Famine (1845–1851) because my initial interest was to document the pre-immigrant lives of Irish people who ended up living in the United States. In the early 1990s, however, the famine was still an extremely touchy subject in Ireland, with many people simply not wishing to hear about it. The history was painful because the times were so horrendous. Millions of families were forced to abandon their homes and property as they were evicted and sent to the United States, Canada, and Great Britain.

It occurred to me that the people living in Ireland today are descended from the survivors and that the evictees' descendants live elsewhere. I suspect that some measure of survivor's guilt may still exist because many families who did not emigrate had to adopt self-serving and often pitiless practices to survive the hunger and disease of those terrible years. The nineteenth century residents of Ballykilcline mentioned in Chapter 1, for example, experienced full-scale eviction during the height of the famine in 1847–1848, leaving only four families in their homes. Those allowed to stay were the families of the Anglican minister and three rent strike informers. This rent strike, its implications, and certainly the famine itself are well remembered locally. I can attest to the unease the descendants of the landlord's agent felt when asked about the evictions, even though they themselves had absolutely nothing to do with them.

What makes the famine a difficult subject in Ireland is its rough contemporaneity with our own times. Though it took place over 150 years ago, its presence is still felt among some people. Their unease reflects the four haunts because the effects of the famine not only existed in the past, but are still very much with us today; they literally *haunt* Ireland. I suspect that this shadowy presence has accounted for the general lack of interest in famine-era archaeology by Irish archaeologists, who are collectively much more interested in ancient history. Many excavators may simply not wish to use archaeology to offer commentaries on our own times or on those that may be easily remembered.

The Special Ability of Modern-World Archaeology

But the point of modern-world archaeology is that historical archaeology, simply because of its close examination of contemporaneity, has a special ability to enlighten us about how our world came to be. Relevant questions abound. Why do we still tolerate colonialist attitudes in the world? Why do so many thousands of people regard capitalist practice as entirely natural? Why do we overlook the expression of rabid Eurocentrism (and Americanism) by prominent commentators and politicians? Why does racialization still exist in liberal democracies? Addressing these questions through the lens of history makes modern-world archaeology relevant as a social practice and bestows special responsibilities upon its practitioners. Given the prominence I assign to relevance, it might be worthwhile to indicate how I came to believe in its importance to historical archaeology.

When I attended college in the late sixties and early seventies, many students and some progressive professors were expressing their concern about whether the social sciences and humanities should be more relevant to society at large. The Port Huron Statement, originally written in 1962—

in Michigan where I lived and attended college—and other left-leaning writings of the 1960s offered provocative statements about reforming the higher education system in the United States. (Students in other countries, notably in France and throughout South America, were engaged in similar pursuits but with significantly more personal risk.) These writings asked questions such as "Is higher education intended only for an elite who would graduate and then serve corporate capitalism, or does a liberal university education have a more profound application, one that could serve a wider citizenry?"

Despite the well-documented elitism and sexism of many in the New Left, their questions nonetheless had resonance—particularly, I believe, for anthropologists. Thoughtful anthropological practice, devoid of its nationalist and collaborationist elements, provided the clear answer: that education should be used for social good or, at a minimum, that its practitioners should appreciate the societal impacts of their efforts. The book *Reinventing Anthropology*, edited by Dell Hymes and published in 1972, helped confirm this for me; but as an archaeologist interested in cultural contact, I could not envision a way in the 1970s to make archaeology relevant. Still, I believed that historical archaeology—because of its subject matter—had inherent relevance to my own times.

In both my master's thesis and doctoral dissertation, I examined how Native Americans adapted to the presence of Europeans and how the foreign objects they incorporated into their cultures could be used to reflect social position and cultural change. In the first case I studied the eighteenth century Michigamea of southern Illinois (who were in contact with French colonists), and in the second the nineteenth century Arikara of South Dakota (who were visited by French, British, and American fur traders and others). I cannot say that I did much to develop the theme of social relevance in either work.

My subsequent research at Millwood Plantation in South Carolina in the early 1980s helped strengthen my understanding of the tenacity of racialization at a postbellum plantation, but the way toward a more socially relevant historical archaeology did not really occur to me until the early 1990s. At this time I was simultaneously developing projects in Brazil (related to slavery and maroonage) and Ireland (concentrated on tenant farming and social revolt). Since after 1865 Millwood Plantation had become a tenant plantation farmed by the estate's former bondsmen and bondswomen, my work there fed quite nicely into both projects.

Thus the research in both Brazil (which concerned the social relations of slavery) and Ireland (which involved the social relations of farm tenancy) was an extension of the program of study I had begun in South Carolina. All three sociohistorical situations were cases where enforced laborers had been "othered" by a class that dominated them economically, politically, racially, and legally. I discovered that though the physical location of my research had changed, the topics I pursued remained remarkably consistent. I could clearly see how seventeenth century Brazil, early nineteenth century Ballykilcline, and nineteenth and early twentieth century Millwood were all connected through certain long-lasting global processes.

Although I have been criticized for observing these links, in my mind the criticisms leveled at modern-world archaeology and its overt interest in acknowledging, understanding, and challenging the four haunts does not lessen their significance during the past five hundred years or make their impacts disappear. Rather, the critics simply demonstrate that the haunts are indeed specters shadowing archaeological practice and that many archaeologists would rather ignore their presence than seek to engage them.

FINAL THOUGHTS

So what modern-world archaeology seeks to do is provide archaeological research on the past five hundred years in such a way that we can easily envision the linkages between the present and the past. Remember that all modern-world archaeology is historical archaeology, but not all historical archaeology is modern-world archaeology. Historical archaeology that is too tightly focused on one short period and one tiny area, and that fails to explore the multiple connections that impacted the individuals living there, is not modern-world archaeology.

At its core modern-world archaeology rests on four pillars that direct its research. The structural history espoused by Braudel and other historians provides a vision of multidimensionality that sees lived history as occurring within a series of frames. These frames can be modeled as vertical (because they exist through time as tradition, custom, and memory) and horizontal (because they exist within the same relative period of time). Network theory helps explain how connections operate across time and space as they simultaneously force us to acknowledge that spaces between individuals, groups, settlements, and artifacts (the links) are every bit as important to the analysis as the things themselves (the nodes).

The careful use of world-systems analysis helps bring diverse elements of the world into sharper focus as an interlinked network directed by managers, agents, and their functionaries across the world since about 1492. One of the key features to remember is that the world changes its shape depending upon the contacts and linkages that are constructed. The "world" in world-systems analysis is not synonymous with the "globe." To understand how to analyze, interpret, and even appreciate how the various disparate elements fit together, we need dialectical thinking. This mode of thought permits us to acknowledge that masters need slaves and that owners need laborers. Any analysis that only focuses on one of these classes necessarily tells an incomplete and thus inaccurate story.

The four pillars provide a guide for investigating the structural processes that have worked together in the world since about 1500. The colonialist urge spread Europeans to all parts of the globe, from the jungles of Southeast Asia to the Peruvian highlands. The perspectives these explorers, missionaries, and merchants took with them were rooted in developing mercantilist ideals. Their perceptions, attitudes, and practices would become the full-blown vulture capitalism in which we are enmeshed today. The systems of inequality fostered by many of the most powerful members of the upper class within each sociohistorical context (whether conquering conquistadors or Boston Brahmins) rested upon foundations of Eurocentrism and racialization. Using clever ideological arguments, the elites in many of the contexts of modern history told many non-elites that they were inherently superior because they had European ancestors and skin colors and other physical features they described as "white." The key to understanding the haunts—their power, appeal, and tenacity—is in recognizing that the haunts have been manipulated as four-quarters of a whole that defines the modern world.

The concept of epochal structures helps us further comprehend how the haunts remain so viable over time. The four substructures represented by the haunts lean upon one another for support and reinforcement. The agents of colonialism use Eurocentrism to enact capitalism, just as capitalists use racialization to argue that only some people deserve to have access to certain commodities. The concept of the epochal structure, though theoretically difficult, is central to understanding how the haunts have remained relevant throughout the past five centuries and why they are still with us today.

Modern-world archaeology, despite its avowed and unapologetic intercontinental vision, does not neglect the local—as some critics have unfairly charged. Quite the contrary, modern-world archaeologists embrace the advances made by microhistorians and fully accept that microarchaeological studies constitute the basics of modern-world archaeology (and all archaeology). But despite the obvious methodological similarities between microhistory and historical archaeology, historical archaeology is not microhistory. The main reason for the difference rests upon archaeology's reliance on artifacts as a primary source of information. The views of archaeologists differ about the theoretical meaning of artifacts, but most of the artifacts in the modern-world must be perceived first and foremost as commodities. As such they have a philosophical distinction from artifacts made by pre-Columbian peoples. This difference helps provide clarity for explaining the diverse values with which commodities can be imbued by their makers and possessors. At their most basic, all artifacts in the modern world are social objects that are acquired as a result of the interaction between taste and economics.

The Challenges Ahead

And finally, modern-world archaeology—in order to become a widely practiced archaeology—must confront a number of challenges. One of the most important challenges is to acknowledge (as many archaeologists are now doing) the separation existing between them, as individuals with privileged educations and opportunities, and the indigenous peoples and descendant communities whom they study. An extremely healthy sign for the future of archaeology appears in the willingness of archaeologists to collaborate with community leaders and keepers of traditional knowledge. I hope that this interest is not simply a fad that disappears over time.

Perhaps the greatest challenge facing modern-world archaeology appears in making the case for acknowledging, understanding, and challenging the four haunts. Postcolonial archaeology is currently leading the way and demonstrating how archaeologists can use their considerable insights for presenting the unvarnished history of the world since about 1500. The same efforts can be made in relation to capitalism, Eurocentrism, and racialization. These cases may be difficult to promote because privileged scholars living in the Western world might find it much more palatable to critique the colonialist practices of the past rather than to interrogate the practices of the other three haunts, especially capitalism. Nonetheless, the challenge remains.

Modern-world archaeology is not easy to practice. In fact, I imagine that it will take some time for its practice to realize its potential. This does not mean, however, that the study of the four haunts should be abandoned or brushed aside. Their union is the great narrative of modern history. No archaeologist really can expect to change history or make the world a better place as a result of excavating a slave quarter, a hunter-collector's fireplace, a farmhouse cellar, a colonial fortification, or the mansion of a tea merchant. But historical archaeologists of the past five centuries have the ability to enlighten us by revealing the true history of the world, and in the process denaturalizing the four haunts. Once denaturalized in history, perhaps their epochal structures might be weakened or changed altogether.

SUGGESTED READINGS

Angelbeck, Bill, and Colin Grier. 2012. Anarchism and the Archaeology of Anarchic Societies: Resistance to Centralization in the Coast Salish Region of the Pacific Northwest Coast. *Current Anthropology* 53:547–587.

Controversial—though very important—new thinking in which archaeologists employ anarchist ideas in their interpretation.

Harrison, Faye V. (editor). 1991. *Decolonizing Anthropology: Moving Further Toward an Anthropology for Liberation*. American Anthropological Association, Washington, DC.
    An important collection that called for postcolonial anthropology. Had an impact on much archaeological thinking.

Hymes, Dell (editor). 1972. *Reinventing Anthropology*. Pantheon, New York.
    A significant assessment of the role of anthropology in the living world. Provided impetus for change in the discipline.

Price, David H. 2004. *Threatening Anthropology: McCarthyism and the FBI's Surveillance of Activist Anthropologists*. Duke University Press, Durham, NC.
Price, David H. 2011. *Weaponizing Anthropology: Social Science in Service of the Militarized State*. CounterPunch, Petrolia, CA.
    Two important, hard-hitting examinations of the ways in which anthropologists and their interpretations can be used in ways they may not imagine. Important object lessons for today's archaeologists.

STUDY QUESTIONS

1. If you believe archaeological research should be relevant to the contemporary world, please give two reasons why. If you do not think so, provide two reasons to support your contention.

2. Explain three ways the actions of governments might affect archaeological practice. For a more in-depth study, outline a real example from the Middle East, Africa, or South America.

3. Why do you think modern-world archaeology has so many challenges? Do the intellectual challenges of working at multiple scales of analysis outweigh the various political challenges that might arise? How might the two intersect?

REFERENCES

Abernethy, David B. 2000. *The Dynamics of Global Dominance: European Overseas Empires, 1415–1980.* Yale University Press, New Haven, CT.

Ashcroft, Bill, Gareth Griffiths, and Helen Tiffin. 1998. *Key Concepts in Post-Colonial Studies.* Routledge, London.

Bentham, Jeremy. 1838. *The Works of Jeremy Bentham, Now First Collected: Under the Superintendence of his Executor, John Bowing, Part I.* William Tait, Edinburgh, UK.

Crockett, David. 1837. *An Account of Col. Crockett's Tour to the North and Down East, In the year of Our Lord One Thousand Eight Hundred and Thirty-Four.* E. L. Carey & A. Hart, Philadelphia.

Davies, Sir John. 1747 [1612]. *A Discoverie of the True Causes Why Ireland Was Never Entirely Subdued.* A. Millar, London.

Eagleton, Terry. 2011. *Why Marx Was Right.* Yale University Press, New Haven, CT.

Ginzburg, Carlo. 1980. *The Cheese and the Worms: The Cosmos of a Sixteenth-Century Miller.* Translated by John Tedeschi and Anne C. Tedeschi. Johns Hopkins University Press, Baltimore, MD.

Hine, Thomas. 2003. *I Want That! How We All Became Shoppers.* Harper-Collins, New York.

Lippert, Dorothy. 2006. Building a Bridge to Cross a Thousand Years. *American Indian Quarterly* 30:431–440.

Locke, John. 1980 [1690]. *Second Treatise of Government.* Edited by C. B. Macpherson. Hackett Publishing, Indianapolis, IN.

Marx, Karl. 1967 [1867]. *Capital: A Critique of Political Economy.* 3 vols. Edited by Frederick Engels. Translated from the Third German Edition by Samuel Moore and Edward Aveling. International Publishers, New York.

Mayhew, Henry. 1861. *London Labour and the London Poor.* 4 vols. Griffin, Bohn & Company, London.

McCracken, Grant. 1990. *Culture and Consumption: New Approaches to the Symbolic Character of Consumer Goods and Activities.* Indiana University Press, Bloomington, IN.

Merwick, Donna. 1999. *Death of a Notary: Conquest and Change in Colonial New York.* Cornell University Press, Ithaca, NY.

Morton, Samuel. 1839. *Crania Americana.* J. Dobson, Philadelphia.

Orser, Charles E., Jr. 1996. *A Historical Archaeology of the Modern World.* Plenum Press, New York.

Orwell, George. 1934. *Burmese Days.* Harper & Brothers, New York.

Orwell. George. 1937. *The Road to Wigan Pier.* Left Book Club, London.

Radcliffe-Brown, A. R. 1940. On Social Structure. *Journal of the Royal Anthropological Society of Great Britain and Ireland* 70:1–12.

Ritzer, George. 2003. *The Globalization of Nothing.* SAIS Review 23:189-200.

Russell-Wood, A. J. R. 1992. *The Portuguese Empire, 1415–1808: A World on the Move.* Johns Hopkins University Press, Baltimore, MD.

Sabloff, Jeremy A. 2008. *Archaeology Matters: Action Archaeology in the Modern World.* Left Coast Press, Walnut Creek, CA.

Schuyler, Robert L. 1970. Historical Archaeology and Historic Sites Archaeology as Anthropology: Basic Definitions and Relationships. *Historical Archaeology* 4:83–89.

Smith, Adam. 1999 [1776]. *The Wealth of Nations.* 2 vols. Edited by Andrew Skinner. Penguin, London.

Trigger, Bruce G. 1980. Archaeology and the Image of the American Indian. *American Antiquity* 45:662–676.

Wakefield, Edward Gibbon. 1849. *A View of the Art of Colonization, With Present Reference to the British Empire.* John W. Parker, London.

INDEX

Abernethy, David, 2
Acculturation, 33, 116
Accumulation of wealth, 18, 32, 77, 80
Acquisition, psychology of, 114–115
Actions
    capitalist, 66
    cultural, 54
    elite controlling, 64–65, 74
    globalized, 34
    human, 47–48, 49, 52, 75
    multidimensional series of, 41
    social, 52
    See also Agency
Activism and activists, 16, 131–132
    See also Legislation, cultural
        preservation
Adaptation, 53, 116
Affluenza, 113
Africa and Africans, 5, 62, 145
    South Africans, 82, 128
    See also Slavery and slaves
African Americans
    archaeology of, 94, 137
    incarceration rate for males, 82
    See also Slavery and slaves
Agency
    historical, 75, 80
    human, 73, 74–77, 79
    See also Actions
American Indian archaeology, 6–7, 14,
    127, 128, 149
    See also Culture contact; Indigenous
        life and peoples
Andros, Edmund, 95
Anglo-Saxon complex, 38–39, 81
Annales d'histoire économique et sociale

(*Annales, Economies, Sociétés, Civi-*
    lizations, journal), 46
Ansell, Christopher, 56
Anthropology
    American, 14, 46, 90, 123, 127
    education in, 57, 130, 147
    Eurocentrism in, 35
    social, 139
Archaeologists and archaeology
    capitalism's linkages to, 26, 129–132
    contemporary, 126–127, 132
    duo-disciplinary approach to, 5–6, 10
    enchantment with objects, 102–105
    feminist, 132
    history of, 88–91
    new ideas in, 126–127
    professionalization of, 25, 94, 130
    relevance of, 146–150
    scale in, 88–91, 96
    separation in, 123, 128–129, 152
    socially responsible, 16, 99
    theory development in, 101, 126
    See also Historical archaeology;
        Modern-world archaeology; *and*
        specific types of archaeology
Arikara tribe (Native Americans), 149
Artifacts, 101–119
    appreciation of, 147
    collectivity of, 114, 115
    Diderot unity of, 113–116
    global spread of, 32
    human relationships with, 102–103,
        105–106, 109–110
    identification of, 7, 127
    interconnectedness of, 61–62, 112–
        113

Artifacts (*cont.*)
  modern-world, 105–108
  multiscalar analysis of, 135–136
  pre-modern distinguished from
      modern, 105–106, 107, 108
  racialization and, 106–107
  as relational objects, 103–105
  social elements of, 17, 104
  taste factor in, 116–118
  thing theory in, 102
  value of, 110–112
  See also Commodities, artifacts as;
      Objects
Ashcroft, Bill, 124
Asia, 36, 62, 63
  See also China; India, trading net-
      works; Japan
Asia : Europe connection, 133–136
Australasian Historical Archaeology
    (journal), 8
Automobile manufacturing, 67
  See also Production

Ballykilcline Society, 13
Ballykilcline townland (Ireland)
  Orser's research in, 11–13, 12*f*, 147–
      148, 149–150
  as social network, 58–59
Behavior, human, 4, 18, 89–90
Bell Beaker phenomenon, 105
Bentham, Jeremy, 126
Blacks. *See* African Americans
Blaut, J. M., 132–133
Bloch, Marc, 46, 121
Bourdieu, Pierre, 32
  habitus concept of, 74, 116–117
Braudel, Fernand
  environmental concept of, 47–48, 51,
      52–53
  Frank's criticisms of, 62, 63
  historical time model of, 45–49
  landscape studies of, 52–53
  multiscalar model of, 49–50, 51, 52–
      53, 64, 88, 91

structural history model of, 47*f*, 49,
    50–51, 70, 150
Braudel, Fernand, writings of *Capital-
  ism and Material Life, 1400–1800,*
    49
  *Civilization and Capitalism: 15th-18th
    Century,* 49
  *The Mediterranean and the Mediter-
    ranean World in the Age of Philip II,*
    46, 48, 49
  *Structures of Everyday Life: The Limits
    of the Possible, The,* 49
Brazil, Orser's studies in, 149–150
Britishness, concept of, 38
    See also England; Ireland

Canada, 7, 8, 13, 148
Capitalism, 29–34
  archaeology's linkages to, 26, 129–
      132
  class and, 38–39
  commodization as element of, 26, 32
  culture of, 30, 32
  in education, 98
  epochal structures of, 84
  examples of, 25–26
  exchange-value in, 111
  feudalism's transformation into, 68
  globalization and, 33–34, 124, 125,
      132, 139
  historical archaeology's study of,
      15–16
  ideologies of, 117–118
  market society, 28–29
  Marx on, 66–69
  mercantilism and, 23, 28–33, 34, 36,
      39–40, 68
  as meta-narrative, 27
  post-1500, 109
  poverty's relationship to, 17
  production and, 31–32, 63, 64, 81,
      107–108
  racialization and, 81, 137–139
  rise of, 77, 105, 126, 151

tea-drinking's impact on, 5
understanding and challenging, 129–132, 141, 152
See also Accumulation, of wealth; Consumerism and consumption; World-economy, capitalist
Capitalist project, 16, 29–34, 66, 67, 68–69, 126
Caravel, Portuguese, development of, 133
Caribbean, 5, 137
Carter, Howard, 5–6
Categories, social, 77–78, 97
Catholicism, 82, 137
Celts, culture of, 38
See also Ireland
Ceramics, 11–12, 33, 108, 133–134, 136
See also Porcelain trade, Chinese
Change
in archaeology, 126, 129, 131, 145
cultural, 15, 33, 127, 149
in epochal structures, 75
global, 62
past, 24, 121
political, 93, 95
in racial definitions, 37
resulting from resistance, 82
situational, 17
societal, 34, 152
temporal, 47, 67, 74, 98
China
culture of, 36
Frank's view of, 62–63, 65
porcelain trade in, 32–33, 34, 62, 133–136
racialization of, 137–138
tea-drinking's origins in, 4–5
China : Japan : Europe network, 135–136
China : Middle East connection, 134
Clans, membership in, 59
See also Groups
Class(es)
capitalist, 38–39, 130

dialectic analysis of, 122–123
hierarchies of, 18
othering by, 149–150
post-medieval, 93
in production, 67–68
race and, 138–139
social position in, 116
struggle for control of, 117
of things, 126
trading, 109–110
in Wallerstein's model, 65
Classical archaeologists, 5–6
Clay pipes, 17, 102*f*
Clothing. *See* Dress
Cohesion, social, 17
See also Groups
Colonial archaeology, 8, 127
Colonialism, 27–29
England's, 30
epochal structures and, 84
Eurocentrism and, 81
European, 28, 124, 151
examples of, 24
imperialism's linkage to, 28–29, 64, 77
mercantilism's linkages to, 28–29
microhistory in, 94–96
modern-world archaeology's study of, 15–16
post-Columbian, 27–28
pre-1945-style, 121–122
processes of, 64, 123–124
silver trade as element of, 135
understanding and challenging, 77, 123, 126
Colonizers : colonized relations, 27, 123
Commercial archaeology, 98, 129, 130, 141
Commodities
acquisition of, 31–32, 32–33, 109
as artifacts, 103–105, 109–110, 112–116, 151
choices of, 116–117

Commodities (*cont.*)
  collectivity, 114
  as element of capitalism, 26, 32
  nature of, 108–110
  value of, 110–112, 116
  worldwide increase in, 104*f*
  See also Consumerism and consumption
Commoners, microhistory of, 10–11, 93–94, 98–99, 117, 151
Communities. *See* Groups
Conjuctures, 48
Connections, 3, 5, 50, 52, 60, 62
  historical, 10, 11, 16, 46, 51
  horizontal and vertical, 54–55, 55*f*, 64
  large-scale, 65–66
  network, 55*f*, 56, 57–58, 59, 61
  political, 63–64
  social, 18, 56, 57, 59
  See also Interconnectedness; Linkages; Modern-world archaeology, the haunts' confluence in; Networks; *and specific connections*
Consumer : seller relations, 32
Consumerism and consumption
  mass, 34, 115–116, 125, 126
  modern-world archaeology's study of, 4, 10, 113, 114–115
  sovereignty of, 117
Core : periphery relations, 64, 66, 121–122
Corporations, 30, 34, 64, 65
  archaeologists employed by, 26, 98, 130, 141
Council for Northeast Historical Archaeology, 8
County Roscommon, Ireland. *See* Ballykilcline townland (Ireland)
Creolization, 33
Crockett, Davy, 139
Culturalist archaeology, 146
Cultural resources, legislation protecting, 26, 130, 141
Culture(s), 18, 54, 97
  African, 145

Asian, 36
capitalist, 30, 32
Celtic, 38
European, 6, 9
Irish, 12–13
non-European, 11
racialization and, 16–17, 137
studies of, 52, 90
uncovering past of, 93–94
See also Acculturation; Eurocentrism; Material culture
Culture contact, 9, 14–16, 17, 114, 122–126, 149
  See also Indigenous life and peoples
Currency, metaphor of, 32
  See also Accumulation of wealth

Davies, Sir John, 28
Debt peonage, 81
  See also Immigrants
Deetz, James, 6
Defoe, Daniel, 32
Delftware, English, 135, 136
Descendant communities, archaeologists collaborating with, 11, 13, 146, 147–148, 152
Determinism, technological, 132–133
Dhow, Arab, development of, 133
Dialectical thinking
  glocalization : grobalization linkages in, 33, 34
  Hegel's, 66–67
  Marx's, 66–69, 70
  in modern-world archaeology, 23, 94, 122–123, 150
  sociospatial, 74
Diderot, Denis, 113–114
Diderot unity, 113–116
Discrimination, 10, 39, 138
  See also Racialization; Racism
Domination, 28, 34
  See also Oppression; Racialization
Donham, Donald, 56, 74–77
Dress, 37, 137
Dutch East India Company, 29

Eagleton, Terry, 69
Economics
  commodity selection and, 103, 116
  market-based, 63, 110–111
  taste's relationship to, 104, 151
  See also Capitalism; Mercantilism;
    World-economy, capitalist
Ecosystems, 51, 53
  See also Environment
Education, archaeological, 32, 98, 130,
  141, 149, 152
Egypt, 5, 16, 107, 132
Elites, 10, 37, 56, 149, 151
  and commodity acquisition, 31–32,
    32–33, 109
  education for, 32, 35, 38, 65, 117
  epochal structures of, 80–81, 82
  frameworks constructed by, 73–75
  southern plantation, 78–79, 83
  tastes of, 117–118
  See also Nonelites
Empires, 29, 63, 77
England, 8, 30
  Anglo-Saxon complex, 38–39, 81
  ceramics industry in, 33, 135, 136
  conflict with the Netherlands, 95–96
  racial issues in, 137, 140
  trading networks in, 54, 62
Enlightenment, European, 35
Enslavers : enslaved relations, 78–79,
  122, 145–146, 150
  See also Slavery and slaves
Environment
  Braudel's concept of, 47–48, 51, 52
  human linkages with, 30, 53, 55, 109
Epochal structures, 73–83
  of capitalism, 84
  of consumption, 116, 117
  elites', 80–81, 82
  of Eurocentrism, 96
  of the haunts, 81–83, 84, 151, 152
  human agency and, 73, 74–77, 99
  Maale people's, 74, 76–77
  resistance to, 114, 118, 122
  of slavery, 80–81

solidity and stability of, 75, 76, 83, 122
Equality, cultural, 35
  See also Inequalities
Ethnicity, 17, 18, 37
Ethnoarchaeology, 127
Ethnocentrism, 16
  See also Eurocentrism
Ethnographers and ethnography, 11–
  13, 35, 82, 90, 93
Eurocentrism, 23, 27, 35–36, 62–63
  epochal structures of, 84, 96
  historical archaeology's bias toward,
    14–15
  nation-states' expression of, 96, 124
  persistence of, 77, 82–83
  racialization and, 36, 38, 77, 81, 124–
    125, 127, 151
  rejection of, 121–122
  understanding and challenging, 132–
    136, 151, 152
European : non-European contact, 9,
  14–18, 114, 122, 125
Europe and Europeans
  archaeology of, 6–7, 8
  culture of, 6, 9
  epochal structures of, 82–83
  exceptionalism in, 35, 132–133
  expansion of, 63, 124, 151
  feelings of superiority on part of, 81,
    125
  feudalism in, 68
  mercantilism in, 28–29, 32, 33, 82
  New, 139
  porcelain trade in, 133–136
  prominence in world history, 62–63
  purported inventiveness of, 132–133
  tea-drinking's impact on, 4–5
  See also individual countries
Excavation(s), 6, 7–8, 10–11, 33, 102*f*
Exceptionalism, 35, 36, 121, 132–133
Exceptional-normal case studies, 94–
  96, 98
Exchange, 15, 64, 109–110, 111–112, 116,
  122

Factories. *See* Automobile manufacturing; Production
Faience ware, 108–109, 133, 136
Febvre, Lucien, 46
  World Destinies (Destins du Monde), 49
Fetishization, 76
Feudalism, 31, 39–40, 68
Frames, 2–5
  analytical, 11, 89, 97–98
  constructed by elites, 74–75
  of epochal structures, 75, 122
  horizontal/vertical, 150
  sliding frame model, 3, 3*f*
France, 46, 117, 136
Frank, Andre Gunder
  on artifacts, 105
  Re-Orient: Global Economy in the Asian Age, 62
  world systems theory of, 61–63, 65
Freedom, 11, 13, 30, 64–65, 73, 117, 123, 130
Future, the, 67, 68

Gender, 16, 65, 76
Geographical time, 47–48, 49, 50–51, 53, 54
  See also Time
Gilded Ages, wealth-poverty gap in, 131
Ginzburg, Carlo, 88, 92–93, 94, 97
Globalization, 33–35, 122
  capitalism and, 33–34, 124, 125, 132, 139
  Chinese, 62–63
  study of, 10, 114
  See Local : global linkages
Glocalization, 33–34
Great Britain. *See* England; Ireland
Great divergence, 7, 123
Great Irish Famine (1845–1851), 11–13, 147–148
Griffiths, Gareth, 124
Grobalization, 33, 34
Groups, 82, 94

interactions of, 51, 53, 55–56, 59
racialization of, 18, 24, 37, 38
  See also Social relations

Habitus, Bourdieu's concept of, 74, 116–117
Hall, James, 7
Hate groups, U.S., 82
  See also Racism
Haunts, the, 23–44
  analyzing, 99, 126
  connections among, 28–29
  epochal structures of, 81–83, 84, 151, 152
  examples of, 24, 25–27
  frameworks of, 73–74
  meaning of, 23–27
  understanding and challenging, 121, 129–140, 148, 151, 152
  See also Capitalism; Colonialism; Eurocentrism; Modern-world archaeology, the haunts' confluence in; Racialization
Hegel, Georg Wilhelm Friedrich, dialectical thinking of, 66–67
Heritage, 18, 38, 137, 146
Hierarchies
  class, 18
  in Maale society, 77
  in plantation society, 78
  racial, 24, 37, 84
  social, 18–19, 32, 37, 64
  vertical linkages of, 53
Hine, Thomas, 115
Historians and history
  of archaeologists and archaeology, 88–91
  from below, 10–11, 93–94, 98–99
  biases in, 48–49
  distinctions between peoples in, 16–17
  modern, 6–7
  object study by, 102–105
  post-Columbian, 41, 65–66, 123, 125–126

structural, 45–51, 70, 150–151
See also Historical time; Microhistory
Historical archaeology
anarchist perspective in, 145
anthropology's relationship to, 15,
46, 90
challenges to, 129, 140–141, 152
conservative nature of, 24, 145
culture contact research, 14–16, 17,
52
definitions of, 5–6, 9
development of, 7–9, 19, 147
Eurocentrism and, 36, 133
great divergence in, 7, 123
microanalysis in, 98–99
microhistory's relationship to, 84,
88–91, 94, 99, 151
modern-world archaeology distinguished from, 1–2, 5–13, 14, 20,
20*t*, 23, 122, 150
multiscalar analysis in, 87–88, 89
post-Columbian, 1, 7, 8–10, 126
prehistoric archaeology distinguished from, 106
racial issues in, 136–40
research themes, 13–19
See also Ballykilcline townland (Ireland); Modern-world archaeology
Historical Archaeology (journal, SHA), 8
Historical time, 45–49, 47*f*, 68, 123
Historic site/sites archaeology, 9–10
Homelessness, studies of, 131–132
Households, network relations between, 64, 65
Housing
plantation, 78*f*, 79, 79*f*, 83
segregation in, 10
Human : artifact relations, 102–103,
105–106, 109–110
Human : ecosystem linkages, 53
Human : environment linkages, 55, 109
Human : human linkages, 30, 52, 53,
55, 109
Human : nature linkages, 30
Human beings

behavior of, 4, 18, 89–90
life of, 51, 68, 97–98, 139, 150
See also Individuals; Lived experi-
ence
Humanistic archaeologists. *See* Particu-
laristic (humanistic) archaeologists
Human-thing entanglement, 102–103
Hybridization, cultural, 33
Hymes, Dell, 149

Idea, the, Hegel's concept of, 66–67
Identity, 17, 18
Immigrants, 38, 52, 81, 137, 139
Imperialism, 28–29, 36, 64, 77, 125
Imperialist archaeology, 15–16, 127
Inarticulate, use of term, 93–94
Independence. *See* Freedom
India, trading networks, 54, 134
Indigenous life and peoples
activists' influencing archaeology of,
128–129, 146
archaeologists' study of, 127, 152
colonialism's effects on, 28, 35
effects on epochal structures, 122
and European contact, 9, 14–16, 17,
33, 149
excavations of, 10–11
globalization process and, 34
See also American Indian archaeology; Culture contact
Individualism, 18, 23, 73, 117–118
Individuals
agency of, 74, 99
dominating, 34
epochal structures and, 82
histories of, 10, 49, 94
interactions of, 30–31, 51, 53, 55–56
isolation of, 76–77
racialization of, 24
See also Human beings
Individual time, 48–49, 66
Industry. *See* Production
Inequalities
class, 151
of colonialism, 27–28

Inequalities (*cont.*)
  in epochal structures, 75, 76, 82, 116,
    118
  race-based, 82
  research on, 14, 16–19, 106
  social, 16–19
  structures of life creating, 51
Inferiority : place linkage, 140
Inquisition, Ginzburg's study of, 92–
    93, 97
Interconnectedness, 1, 52, 112–113,
    122–123
  See also Connections; Networks
*International Journal of Historical Archae-
    ology* (journal), 8
Ireland, 30, 137–138
  See also Ballykilcline townland (Ire-
    land)
Italy, pottery in, 133, 136

Jamestown, Virginia, excavation at, 8
Janse van Ilpendam, Adriaen, Mer-
    wick's study of, 95–96, 97, 98, 99
Japan, 108, 135–136
Jefferson, Thomas, 25

Kiddey, Rachael, 131
Kings, divine right of, 75
  See also Power
King Tut's tomb, discovery of, 5
Kinship connections, 59
  See also Connections; Groups
Krober, A. L., 46

Labor
  divisions of, 76, 109–110
  valuing, 78–79, 81, 111
  See also Wages
Laborers : owners relations, 32, 150
Landscape studies, Braudel's use of,
    52–53
Language, 16, 96, 128, 137, 138
Las Casas, Bartolomé de, 28, 126
Left Book Club, 139

Legislation, cultural preservation, 26,
    130, 141
Linkages
  historical, 62, 70, 150
  network, 54*f*
  physical, 59–61
  structural nature of, 18
  theory of, 66
  See also Connections; Networks;
    Nodes; *and specific linkages*
Lippert, Dorothy, 25–26
Lived experience, 45, 67, 97–98, 150
Local : global linkages, 1, 2–5, 26
  Ballykilcline example, 12–13
  in Braudel's model, 51, 70
  dialectics of, 69, 94
  historical archaeology's study of, 11,
    14, 88–89, 151
  in Janse example, 96, 98–99
  See also Globalization; Glocalization
Locke, John, 28
Lowie, Robert, 46

Maale people (Ethiopia), 56, 74, 76–77
Macroanalysis, 91, 93, 113
Marketing, 33, 64
  See also Consumerism and consump-
    tion
Market society, 28–29, 30
  See also Capitalism; Mercantilism
Martin, Félix, 7
Marx, Karl
  on capitalism, 30–31, 63, 66–69, 130,
    131
  on commodities, 109, 110
  on dialectical thinking, 66–69, 70
  on mercantilism, 28–29, 31
  on spectre haunting Europe, 24
  on value, 29, 111
Mary, Queen (England), 32–33
Material culture, 66, 118, 124
  archaeological theories regarding, 50,
    101
  assemblages of, 137–138

European, 132–133
multiculturism in, 133–136
research on, 98–99, 103
taste's role in, 104
See also Commodities; Culture(s);
  Objects
Mayhew, Henry, 138
McCracken, Grant, 113, 114
McGuire, Randall, 130
Medici, Cosimo de', 56
Menocchio, Ginzburg's study of, 92–
  93, 94, 97, 98, 99
Mercantilism
  capitalism and, 23, 28–33, 34, 36, 39–
    40, 68
  ideologies of, 117–118
  Portuguese, 133, 134
  post-1500, 82, 109
  poverty's relationship to, 17
  rise of, 105, 108, 151
  tea-drinking's impact on, 4–5
Merwick, Donna, 94–96, 97
Metals, precious, 110–111, 134–135
Meta-narratives, 26–27
Meta-processes, the haunts as, 24, 26–
  27
Mexico, potters in, 135
Michigamea tribe (Native Americans),
  149
Microanalysis, 91–92, 93, 94, 98–99, 113
Microarchaeology, 151
Microhistory, 87–100
  colonial America and, 94–96
  essences of, 91–98
  exceptional-normal case studies in,
    94–96, 98
  Ginzburg's, 92–93
  historical archaeology's relationship
    to, 84, 88–91, 94, 98–99, 151
  lower orders and, 93–94, 139
  modern-world archaeology and, 87–
    88
  multiscalar analysis and, 94, 97–98
  pitfalls of, 98–99

social networks and, 97–98
Stewart's, 91–92
Middle East : Asia connections, 133–
  136
Middle East, trade in, 62, 133, 134
Millwood Plantation (South Carolina),
  149–150
Ming Dynasty (China), 62, 134
Modern history, use of term, 6–7
Modernity, 26, 105, 126
  critique of, 9–10
  Diderot unity as feature of, 115–116
  universalist ideology of, 65, 69
Modern-world archaeology
  artifacts of, 105–108, 151
  challenges to, 121–143, 152
  definitions of, 1–2, 9
  development of, 19–20
  dialectical thinking in, 23, 94, 122–
    123, 150
  Diderot unity in, 113–116
  foundational pillars of, 45, 69–70,
    150–151
  future of, 145–152
  goals of, 9–11, 57, 84
  the haunts' confluence in, 27, 36, 38,
    39–41, 40*f*, 77, 124, 129–140, 141
  historical archaeology distinguished
    from, 1–2, 5–13, 14, 20, 20*t*, 23,
    122, 150
  interconnectedness in, 1, 52, 112–113,
    122–123
  microhistory and, 87–88
  poverty studies, 17–19
  relevance of, 26, 146–150
  scope of, 1, 4, 11, 87
  separation in, 128–129, 152
  subject matter of, 39–41
  See also Ballykilcline townland (Ire-
    land); Haunts, the; Historical ar-
    chaeology; Multiscalar analysis
Monetary (Mercantile) System, 31
Money, 32, 117
Morton, Samuel, 37

Muffled inclusiveness, 38
Multiculturalism, 36, 125–126, 133–136
Multidimensionality, 41, 52, 59, 64, 150
Multiscalar analysis
    Braudel's model of, 47, 47f, 49–50, 51,
        52–53, 64
    in historical archaeology, 68, 87–88
    in Maale society, 77
    microhistory and, 94, 97–98
    in modern-world archaeology, 1, 15,
        51, 57, 70, 97–98, 125, 133
    of poverty, 18–19
    See also Ballykilcline townland (Ire-
        land)

Nationalism, 8, 127, 145
Nationalist archaeology, 146
Nation-states, 18, 34, 64, 140
    European, 126, 133
    expressions of Eurocentrism in, 96,
        124
Native Americans : Europeans link-
    ages, 149
Native peoples. See American Indian
    archaeology; Culture contact; In-
    digenous life and peoples
Nature. See Environment
Ndlovu, Ndukuyakhe, 128
Neoliberalism, 73
Netherlands, the
    conflict with England, 95–96
    porcelain trade in, 62, 134–135, 136
Network relations, 56, 64, 93, 133–134
    See also Relationships; Social rela-
        tions
Networks
    artifacts functioning within, 61–62,
        112–113
    boundaries of, 97–98, 99
    capitalist, 30–31
    global, 33–34
    the haunts and, 24, 40, 41
    horizontal/vertical linkages in, 24,
        27, 40, 53–56, 54f, 68, 75, 97–99,
        150

household, 64, 65
of interaction, 52–53
multiscalar, 52, 77
sociospatial, 55–56, 57, 60, 64–65
spatial, 58, 59, 70
theory of, 51–61
trading, 54, 107
trans-temporal, 67, 126
units of analysis in, 57–60
See also Connections; Interconnected-
    ness; Linkages; Nodes; Social net-
    work theory; Space, horizontal
    linkages in; Time, vertical link-
    ages in
New Deal programs, archaeological, 8
New Left, 149
New York, 10, 12
    See also Janse van Ilpendam, Adri-
        aen, Merwick's study of
Nodes, 54f, 62, 66, 70, 150
    See also Networks
Nomothetic archaeologists, 89–90
Noncapitalist societies, 29, 32, 76, 116
    See also Capitalism
Nonelites, 10–11, 93–94, 99, 117, 151
    See also Elites
Non-European peoples, 81, 125, 133
    See also American Indian archaeol-
        ogy; Culture contact; European :
        non-European contact; Indige-
        nous life and peoples
North America, 5–6, 14, 34, 109–110,
    114–115, 132
    See also American Indian archaeol-
        ogy; Mexico, potters in; United
        States (U.S.)

Objects
    archaeology's enchantment with, 14,
        102–105
    artifacts as relational, 103–105, 151
    exchange value of, 111–112
    linkages through time, 50, 54–55
    modern vs. pre-modern, 104, 105–106

See also Artifacts; Commodities; Things

Ollman, Bertell, 66

Opposites, union of, 34
See also Dialectical thinking

Oppression, 16, 37, 65
See also Domination; Racialization

Orwell, George, 36
Road to Wigan Pier, The, 139–140

Other, the
class distinctions creating, 149–150
racialization of, 117, 137–138

Ottoman Empire, potters in, 135

Padgett, John, 56

Park Avenue: Money, Power, and the American Dream (film, Gibney), 131

Particularistic (humanistic) archaeologists, 90, 98–99, 127, 145

Past : present linkages
in African archaeology, 128
frames in, 3–4
in historical archaeology, 13, 99, 127
in modern-world archaeology, 10, 122, 125, 131–132, 150
See also Historical time; Networks, trans-temporal; Time, vertical linkages in

Patrimony, cultural, 16, 128

Peasants, study of, 11–12, 31
See also Feudalism; Tenant farmers

Peoples, study of, 16–17, 50, 60
See also American Indian archaeology; Elites; Human beings; Indigenous life and peoples; Nonelites

Physical appearance, race defined as differences in, 16–17, 137, 138–139, 140

Plantations, U.S., study of, 77–81, 78*f,* 79*f,* 83, 149–150

Plato, dialectical thinking of, 66

Politics, 16, 59, 63–64, 129

Poor people, 32, 36, 131, 137, 139
See also Poverty

Porcelain trade, Chinese, 32–33, 34, 62, 133–136
See also Ceramics

Port Huron Statement (1962), 148–149

Portugal, 82, 133
porcelain trade in, 62, 134, 135, 136

Postcolonial archaeology, 145, 152

Postcolonialism, 123–127
defining, 124–125
elements of analysis, 125–126
historical archaeology's study of, 15–16
new ideas in, 126–127
post-colonial distinguished from postcolonial, 123
rise of, 129

Post-medieval archaeology, 8

Postmodernism/post-modernity, 9, 26

Pottery, production of, 107–108, 133–134
See also Porcelain trade, Chinese

Poverty
archaeological study of, 131–132, 146
racialization and, 17–19, 137–38, 139–140
See also Poor people

Power
elites', 56, 82
epochal structures of, 75, 84
purchasing, 116–117
relations of, 59, 116
taste and, 117–118

Prehistoric archaeology, 106, 109

Privileges, 29, 116, 146

Processes, dialectical relations as, 67
See also Metaprocesses, the haunts as

Production
capitalist, 31–32, 63, 64, 81, 107–108
class involved in, 67–68
in Maale society, 76
See also Workers : owners relations

Race
definitions of, 16, 24
ethnicity distinguished from, 18, 37

Race (*cont.*)
  in historical archaeology, 136–140
  inequalities caused by, 82
  physical appearance as basis for, 16–
      17, 137, 138–139, 140
  poverty's relationship to, 17–19
Racialization, 23, 27, 37–39
  artifacts and, 106–107
  capitalism and, 81, 137–138
  Eurocentrism and, 36, 38, 77, 81, 124–
      125, 127, 151
  examples of, 10, 24
  understanding and challenging, 122–
      123, 126, 136–140, 149–150, 152
  in U.S., 18, 37–38, 77–81, 124
  See also Domination; Oppression
Racism, 38, 39, 65
  epochal structures and, 82–83, 84
  See also Discrimination
Radcliffe-Brown, A. R., 52
Rationality, 35
Ravensteyn, Hubert van, *Still Life of a
    Flower, Glass, Stoneware Jug, and
    Walnuts in a Chinese Bowl on a Ledge*
    (painting, van Ravensteyn), 135
Rebellions, 64–65, 73, 122
Relational thinking, 66
  See also Dialectical thinking
Relationships, 74, 103–105, 109–110
  See also Network relations; Social
      relations
Religion, 52, 82, 83, 137
Rent strike, Ballykilcline, Ireland, 11–
    13, 148
Research, archaeological, 88–89, 125,
    132
Resistance, 64, 118
  change resulting from, 82, 122
  indigenous peoples', 16, 17, 36
Rich : poor gap, 131
Ritzer, George, 34
Ruled : ruler relations, 59
Russell-Wood, A. J. R., 122

Sabloff, Jeremy, 126
Scale, in archaeology, 89–91, 96
Scandella, Domenico. *See* Menocchio,
    Ginzburg's study of
Schliemann, Heinrich, 5–6, 25
Scholars and scholarship, 16, 129, 132–
    133
  See also Education, archaeological;
      Research, archaeological
Scholfield, John, 131–132
Schuyler, Robert, 6, 9, 90
Scientific archaeology, 89–91
Segregation, 10
  See also Discrimination; Racism
Separation, 123, 128–129, 152
Serf : lord relations, 31
  See also Feudalism
Settlements
  historical archaeology's study of, 14,
      52, 53, 90
  racial classification's relationship to,
      10
  See also Ballykilcline townland (Ire-
      land); Plantations, U.S., study of
Sexism, 65, 149
Shopping. *See* Consumerism and con-
    sumption
Silver, Spanish trade in, 134–135
Single-site archaeology, 11, 15, 88, 141,
    145
Site-specific archaeology, 60–61, 62, 87,
    89, 90–91, 97–98
Slavery and slaves
  epochal structures in, 80–81
  linkages to, 5, 60
  social relations of, 149–150
  U.S., 11, 12, 25, 37–38, 77–80, 83
  See also Enslavers : enslaved relations
Sliding frame model, 3, 3*f*
Smart phones, 4, 5
Smith, Adam
  on colonialism, 28
  on commodities, 109, 110
  on exchange value, 111–112

on mercantilism, 31–32
Social Darwinism, 35
　See also Eurocentrism
Socialism, 67, 68
　See also Marx, Karl
Socialization, process of, 64–65, 116
Social network theory, 52, 53–56, 57–58,
　70, 93, 97–98
　See also Networks
Social relations, 56–57
　of capital, 30, 32
　in epochal structures, 73–74, 76
　hierarchical, 18–19
　in Maale society, 77
　of slavery, 79, 149–150
　See also Groups; Network relations;
　　Relationships
Social sciences, historical interpreta-
　tion's connections to, 51, 103
Social status, 17
Social time, 48, 49, 51, 66
　See also Time
Society for Historical Archaeology
　(SHA), 8
Society for Post-Medieval Archaeology
　(SPMA), 8
Socioeconomics, 17
　See also Economics
South America, 57, 62, 116, 132, 149
Space
　of epochal structures, 84
　expression of the haunts in, 141
　geographical, 1, 48, 54
　horizontal linkages in, 33, 53, 55f, 131
　of modern-world archaeology, 40f
Spain
　rise and fall of empire in, 62
　trade by, 134–135, 136
Specific : general linkages, in Braudel's
　model, 51
Standish, Miles, excavation of home
　site, 7
States (political entities), 65

Ste. Marie I mission (Ontario), excava-
　tion of, 7
Stewart, George R., 91–92
*Still Life of a Flower, Glass, Stoneware
　Jug, and Walnuts in a Chinese Bowl on
　a Ledge* (painting, van Ravensteyn),
　135
Structures, 73–85
　Braudel's research on, 48, 50–51
　dual, 80–81
　epochal, 73–83
　of poverty, 18–19
　southern plantation, 77–81, 83, 149–
　　150
　See also Historians and history, struc-
　　tural

Taste, 104, 116–118, 151
Tea-drinking, global ramifications of,
　4–5, 32–33, 117–118
Temporal : spatial linkages, 50
Tenant farmers, 11–13, 149–150
　See also Peasants
Text-aided archaeology, 5–6
Things
　class of, 126
　human-thing entanglement, 102–103
　as material culture component, 4, 10,
　　50
　racialization and access to, 106–107
Third Anglo-Dutch War of 1673, 95
Third World, 28, 61
Tifflin, Helen, 124
Time
　Braudel's model of, 45–49, 47f
　of epochal structures, 84
　expression of the haunts in, 141
　vertical linkages in, 33, 54–55, 55f,
　　131
　See also Geographical time; Great di-
　　vergence; Historical archaeology;
　　Individual time; Networks, trans-
　　temporal; Social time

Tin-glazed earthenware, myth of, 133–
    136
Tourism, archaeology's promotion of,
    8, 13, 83, 146
Trade and traders
    beginnings of, 30, 107, 108–110
    England's monopoly of, 36, 54
    global, 29, 33
    international, 110–111, 114
    porcelain, 32–33, 34, 62, 133–136
Traditional historical archaeology. *See*
    Historical archaeology
Treaty of Breda (1667), 95
Treaty of Westminster (1674), 95
Trigger, Bruce, 126–127, 128
Troy, discovery of, 6, 25

United States (U.S.)
    Anglo-Saxon complex, 39
    colonial microhistory, 94–96
    exceptionalism in, 35
    historical archaeology in, 7–8, 145
    immigrant influx, 38, 137
    poverty in, 18–19, 139
    racialization in, 18, 37–38, 77–81, 124
    slavery in, 11, 12, 25, 37–38
    See also Plantations, U.S., study of
Universalism, 65
Universalized : particular relations, 69
    See also Dialectical thinking
Universities
    business model adopted by, 130
    elite, 32, 35, 38, 65, 117
    See also Education, archaeological
Urban areas, 64, 138, 139

Value
    of commodities, 110–112
    esteem, 111–112
    exchange, 111–112, 116
    Marx on, 29
    use, 111–112
Violence, 28, 29, 39

Wages, 30, 32, 130
    See also Labor, valuing
Wakefield, Edward Gibbon, 27
Wallerstein, Immanuel, world-
    systems theory of, 61, 63–65,
    65–66, 70, 91, 106
Wanli pattern, porcelain, 135
Wealth, 130, 131
    accumulation of, 18, 32, 77, 80
West, the. *See* Europe and Europeans;
    United States (U.S.)
Whites, 38, 77–78, 137, 151
Workers : owners relations, 31, 59, 67,
    122
    See also Production
Working-class, racialization of, 138–
    139
World-economy, capitalist, 62–65, 69–
    70
World-systems analysis, 87, 88, 90,
    150
    Frank's, 61–63, 65
    Wallerstein's, 63–65, 65–66, 70, 106
Worldviews, 48, 70

Zimmerman, Larry, 128, 131–132